SURVIVING CHURCH CONFLICT

SURVIVING CHURCH CONFLICT

Dave Peters

HERALD PRESS
Scottdale, Pennsylvania
Waterloo, Ontario

Library of Congress Cataloging-in-Publication Data
Peters, Dave, 1949-
  Surviving church conflict / Dave Peters.
    p. cm.
  Includes bibliographical references.
  ISBN 0-8361-9051-3 (alk. paper)
  1. Church controversies. 2. Conflict management—Religious
aspects—Christianity. I. Title.
BV652.9.P48 1997
331.7—dc21

96-40869

The paper used in this publication is recycled and meets the minimum
requirements of American National Standard for Information Sciences
—Permanence of Paper for Printed Library Materials, ANSI Z39.48-
1984.

All Bible quotations are used by permission, all rights reserved, and
unless otherwise indicated are from the *New Revised Standard Version
Bible,* copyright 1989, by the Division of Christian Education of the
National Council of the Churches of Christ in the USA.

SURVIVING CHURCH CONFLICT
Copyright © 1997 by Herald Press, Scottdale, Pa. 15683
    Published simultaneously in Canada by Herald Press,
    Waterloo, Ont. N2L 6H7. All rights reserved
Library of Congress Catalog Number: 96-40869
International Standard Book Number: 0-8361-9051-3
Printed in the United States of America
Book and cover design by James Butti

06 05 04 03 02 01 00 99 98 97 10 9 8 7 6 5 4 3 2 1

———————

To my wife, Barbara,
who has faithfully served the Lord
and loved me in difficult places of service;
a faithful pastor's wife,
serving the churches of the Lord,
bringing God's love to many people,
and fostering reconciliation among members

Contents

CHAPTER THREE

CHAPTER FOUR

Foreword

In some ways the church is analogous to Noah and the ark. If it weren't for the storm outside, one wouldn't be able to stand the stench inside. Or to put it another way, conflict in the church is inevitable. The following is evidence of this:

Adam and Eve experienced conflict.
Abraham and Sarah grew through conflict.
Joshua and Caleb experienced conflict.
David's life was filled with conflict.
The prophets abounded in conflict.
The Lord Jesus went to the cross over conflict.
The New Testament claims conflict is essential for growth.
(James 1:2-4, NIT)

Therefore, one needs to view church conflict and its resolution as a "personal adventure into spiritual growth and development" (p. 85). In the heat of conflict, the Christian can find joy in knowing that it is a part of God's plan to build his people into persons suitable to inhabit eternity with him.

The New Testament church in the book of Acts is often placed on a pedestal as exemplary, and rightfully so. However, this pristine church had its problems, as noted especially in Acts 5, 6, and 15.

Conflict in the church guarantees that the church will never be the same thereafter. These are moments that serve as journey markers along the way.

The author, from a broad and varied experience, firmly believes that the solution to such problems in the church requires a biblical base. His threefold approach shows this.

The first is a reliance upon God's grace. He says, "Human methodology can never supersede or replace divine involvement" (p. 147). We must recognize that God is in the midst of even an experience of conflict in the church. Apart from his grace and an appreciation of it, there can be no resolution. This applies to all sides in the conflict.

Next, the rule of Christ in Matthew 18, the authors says, gives the outline for the biblical process. The intent and purpose is reconciliation, reconciliation, and reconciliation. This calls for submission to one another instead of operating from a position of strength.

Third, the author calls for peacemaking. It is good to find one who applies Ephesians 6:10-18 to the church rather than to the individual: the church should "put on the whole armor of God." After all, this application is certainly to be preferred in a letter called the "ecclesiological epistle."

The church in conflict is like Peter, who stepped over the side of the boat into a raging sea when Jesus said "Come" (Matt. 14:29). Jesus has called his followers to come. Conflict is raging all about. Conflict is inevitable. Conflict cannot be avoided if we are to follow Jesus. Jesus beckons us to come and walk with him through it. But like Peter, the church sometimes takes her eyes off the Lord when confronted by the reality of the raging conflict and the fear of what might happen. At this point, the church begins to sink. As with Peter, there is only one hope, and that is to call out to the Lord, "Save me."

When facing conflict in the church, God's grace is sufficient. The rule of Christ is adequate, and peacemaking is a necessity.

—*Richard E. Allison, Dean*
  Ashland (Ohio) Theological Seminary

Preface

I have always hated violence, whether it involved the ill treatment directed toward the neighbor's howling dog or the bully who pesters the kid down the street. We live in a violent world. Violence intrudes into every life, creating misery and pain.

All my life I have been in a battle against violence. I have been victimized, and regrettably I have caused it. Each day I submit to the call of Jesus Christ upon my life. That is an offensive against violence. It is more than my personal management of my life and faith with a hope to minimize the effects of violence.

This book shows that Jesus Christ has come as the Prince of Peace to defeat violence. This book shows how to conquer the debilitating effects of conflict and violence. It is designed to provide layman and clergy some direction needed for standing up against the darts of evil, and to triumph over the devil's schemes.

In several pastoral assignments, I had the privilege of providing leadership to congregations that were in conflict before I arrived there. In my pastoral ministry, I began a search for ways to end conflict. The search continued for nearly two decades. Whenever someone would mention a method to produce unity, I would listen intently. Eventually I realized what I knew all along, that the only solution to problem solving is what is found in the Scriptures. This book is a re-examination of scriptural solutions to conflict resolution. The church today needs to revisit these scriptural teachings.

My thanks are extended to those who have tolerated my own

personal naïveté and stumbling as I searched for answers concerning conflict resolution. To the churches I have pastored both in the United States and Canada, to the colleagues that have critically offered their advice and love, to those who disagreed with me, to my denominational leaders in the Evangelical Friends Church, Eastern Region, who have mutually searched for ways to provide for a unified and loving church—to all those I offer my thanks and appreciation.

I would also be remiss if I did not thank my mentor and friend in the ministry Rev. L. Frank Willoughby of the Church of the Nazarene. His love and spiritual insight painfully forced me to grow beyond myself into servanthood before Christ at a depth previously unknown to me. But most of all, I am grateful to my Lord Jesus Christ, who has kept me near his heart when the ways of life were unclear.

—*Dave Peters*

CHAPTER ONE

Restoration of the Church in Crisis

Introduction

It is heartbreaking to discover that our best attempts to foster church unity and love among members can be a failure. Suddenly, within the circumstances of the local church, we may find ourselves dreaming of former years when brothers and sisters were bonded together in the joy of Christ. We sit in our habitual corner of the meetinghouse, in a pew no longer warm. The room is now filled with tearful confusion and anger. Division has broken the bond of peace. Dissension has caused bitterness to sprout and take root among those who formerly were our friends and companions in the kingdom.

The word *formerly* seems so final in its interpretation. Yet church members can shockingly discover themselves unable to love as they used to love. In the deep inward pain of church division, the joyous relationship with God can become fogged in by the human hurts we experience when the chosen of the Lord do not behave as the Lord's chosen ones. The church is no longer the same.

Pastors and laypersons alike have become grieved over church division. A pastor in the midst of church division felt the pangs of discouragement when he failed to end the warfare in the church. He said, "I no longer want to live. I can't go on. I pray each day that the Lord will take me. I have thought of suicide. The only driving force that keeps me going is this question: Who will take care of my family?" Another pastor reported, "My own self-image is shattered. I feel like a total failure. Although I never believed that God had abandoned me, I felt as though he had. I can't sense any closeness or any direction or leading from God. I often want to run away—anywhere!"

These responses are similar to the frustration experienced by the apostle Paul as he wrote to the Corinthian church: "We do not want you to be unaware, brothers and sisters, of the affliction we experienced in Asia; for we were so utterly, unbearably crushed that we despaired of life itself" (2 Cor. 1:8). Such responses reflect intense strains in the lives of two professional pastors and of the apostle Paul. Yet they are like what dedicated laypeople may express in the pain of conflict.

In one congregation where the pastor had been voted out, a division was apparent when those loyal to him objected to a new pastoral candidate. After much discussion and tears, members came to a consensus, but the disunity from the previous pastoral conflict was evident. Church members referred to that meeting in negative terms for a long time afterward, hoping they would never again have to go through pastoral problems of such magnitude. Bitterness and various misunderstandings were the result of that conflict among Christians. The church was left socially and spiritually divided.

In one church, members noticed a decline in Sunday morning attendance. When this occurred, a cloud of depression hovered over those who had decided to remain in the congregation. After they covenanted with a new pastor, the intensity of the problem increased when they discovered that people were *still* leaving the church.

Why do people leave a congregation? Often there are many unanswered questions about this that discourage God's people. Do they leave because of guilt from their own involvement in the conflict? Because of social pressure in the church which makes it difficult for them to leave earlier in the conflict? Do they leave due to their own personal inability to adjust to new or old pastoral leadership? Does their own carnality and secret sin make them feel out of place when the majority of the congregation is reconciled with each other and with God? Do they leave because they feel isolated from primary social contacts who have already left the church? Because they are now in unreconcilable conflict with those in the congregation who formerly were their trusted friends? Such a list of questions could be extended indefinitely.

The Corinthian church is a prime example of a church in crisis. These house-church believers were in the midst of tense chaos. To understand their circumstances, hurts, and efforts to resolve conflict, we need to view them as more than just items of the past. We must visualize them as those for whom Christ gave his life (1 Cor. 8:11). The Christians at Corinth were not pagans whose every action was outrageous barbarity. These were believers who had been torn inwardly by confusion and outwardly by conflict. They found themselves between the proverbial rock and a hard place. Believers had to reckon with the social pressure of an immoral society hostile to the gospel of Christ if they were to demonstrate genuine faith in the life of the church.

In the Corinthian church and in many congregations today, there are members who, in response to church tensions, give up their spiritual journey with Christ. Others, in the middle of problems, simply want to be left alone. In a divided church, people often can no longer trust each other well. The caring ministry of the church may be criticized and belittled because of personal hurts that have overwhelmed people. In the church today, pastoral changes can be viewed either as the solution to the problem or as an added burden for the congregation. No doubt a similar reaction occurred at Corinth, when Paul left and then Apollos arrived. The change in leadership may or may not provide the church fresh opportunities to experience a renewed sense of vision and reconciliation among factions in the church.

When a congregation feels forced to remove a pastor from a leadership role, they may lose an opportunity for fostering reconciliation within the body of Christ. They may also neglect the root causes of the division and bring nothing but astonishment as pastors depart, one after another. A stopgap attempt (change of pastors) may bring some relief from the tension. However, when only part of the situation is addressed and the remainder is neglected, a relapse into the original problem will likely occur. This will produce even greater strain on the congregation when they begin wondering what is so wrong with them. Then they become more depressed, feeling overwhelmed by not being able to address the facts truthfully and straightforwardly.

In the Corinthian letters, the apostle Paul is under severe scrutiny by his opponents, who want to control the church. Their ambition is to ruin his reputation in the church. Paul responds to them by directing the congregation to a full allegiance to the living God. He demands that they separate themselves from worldly desires (2 Cor. 6:14—7:1).

We need to think soberly about the frailty of people who, to resist and protect themselves from the hurt of broken relationships, will choose to leave the congregation. These people are not necessarily cowards in the faith. They are not necessarily uncommitted. They are wounded and need healing in a church atmosphere that is increasingly violent.

For example: Mrs. A, when leaving the church for the last time, commented that no one cared if her family attended the church or not. It is true that few did care, due to her obnoxious behavior over a period of years and especially during a recent church crisis. Her wounds in the struggle and her invective toward others had smothered the congregation's effort to be a church family for her. In the bitterness that had infected her life, she had lost the ability to perceive the love that others desperately wanted to develop and share with her. Finally, to protect their own emotional needs, people began to shun her because she had repeatedly hurt the feelings of others in the church.

When Mrs. A's family left, someone commented to the new pastor that now the biggest hindrance to their own attendance in the church was gone. With the departure of the A's, a sense of peace came into the church. The cost of this peace, whether permanent or temporary, was the loss of a family to the congregation. The price of peace is high and sometimes quite costly. The removal of a person or family from the life of the church is a serious undertaking. It must never be taken lightly.

The apostle Paul, burdened with love and responsibility, was faced with a situation at Corinth involving the sin of a man who was having a sexual relationship with his stepmother. Paul instructed the church to remove the man from their fellowship and to turn him over to Satan for the destruction of his flesh, so that his spirit might be saved (1 Cor. 5:1-5). The outcome of church discipline, declared officially or unofficially, may seem at first to be harsh and cruel. However, many pastors and laypeople have found the flip side so true. Sin, if allowed to continue in any congregation, will eventually destroy the spiritual vitality of the church.

In another case of discipline, Paul instructs the church that the punishment inflicted upon a (former) member is sufficient. They are now to restore the man to the fellowship of the church (2 Cor. 2:5-11). Mrs. A and her family became the product of unofficial church discipline due to her bitter spirit. She had become her own worst enemy. Church discipline must always be redemptive. By her own attitude, Mrs. A refused the redemptive side of church discipline.

The man in the church who was having a sexual relationship with his father's wife apparently was not redeemed by the church discipline inflicted upon him (unless 2 Cor. 2:5-11 refers to him). There are always those who choose to do sinful things and consequently fail to enter into the peace of Christ. Sometimes they feel that if they can just get away from the pressure, then they will be at peace. They may believe that what they do in secret is no one's business but their own. This is not true. Sin will continue to destroy any unrepentant sinner. Peace and cohesiveness within the church demands holy living and church discipline with love. There are no private or secret sins. Unrepentant sin affects everyone.

It is always a tragedy when discipline fails to be redemptive. Mrs. A lost out when she failed to receive redemptive church discipline. The church lost out when it failed to confront her with her sins. They both lost the opportunity to restore her relationship with the church and with the Lord Jesus Christ. The A's resettled in another church, where similar problems have again developed. Churches often hope that mistakes of the past won't be repeated in the future, but that is merely wishful thinking unless needed changes are made.

In every issue of church conflict, there are always special circumstances totally unique to the local congregation. It is often difficult to judge things that only the mind of Christ knows and has not yet revealed to his church. In any study of conflict resolution, there must be an understanding that no two churches are exactly alike. However, the constant truth in all conflict is that sin is ugly and deadly. Where there is conflict, sin is knocking at the door. How we respond to each other in conflict is important.

Paul speaks about the difference Christ makes on the church. The church is not to live like the world. Paul sets the standard for all God's people, telling them how to live each day (Col. 3:1-17). "If you have been raised with Christ, seek the things that are above, where Christ is, seated at the right hand of God. Set your minds on things that are above, not on things that are on earth" (Col. 3:1-2). Paul wants the Colossians to understand that Christianity is a religion of the heart. If the condition of the heart is evil, then the light by which each must walk is faint.

We have been "hidden with Christ in God" (Col. 3:3). Christ has become our life. The heart must be changed, or there will be no evidence of a changed life. We are told to change our hearts before we are told to change our minds. There is no point in changing a mind if the heart is set on living in sin. The heart must be changed first, and this can only be done when the heart is set first on Christ.

The darkened mind and heart cannot see the greatness of life as God sees it. We need to view life as God sees it. We must have his perspective. The heart and mind must be transformed by the grace of God. Only then do we discover each day his perfect will for our lives. When the heart is right with God, then and only then can we put to death the earthly nature. We set our minds on the eternal things of God because in them we find life. We are warned to get rid of such things as anger, wrath, malice, slander, abusive and filthy language, and lying (Col. 3:8-9). We are to put on a new self which is constantly being renewed in knowledge according to the image of God (Col. 3:10).

The church is to be God's holy people. Members are to have the qualities of compassion, kindness, humility, meekness, and patience. They are to bear with one another and to forgive each other. The church is to be filled with love (Col. 3:12-14). This is in stark contrast to the worldlings, who live in sin. Paul states that such are the enemies of the cross. Their destiny is destruction. Their God is their belly. They glory in their shame. Their minds are on earthly things. They do not have citizenship in heaven (Phil. 3:17-20).

In conflict resolution, we need to remember that there is a spiritual battle going on between the holy and unholy. The church is called to conform to the holy. That can be done only through costly struggle.

The conflict at Corinth left the apostle Paul emotionally wounded. We must wonder how his wounds affected his perspective of himself and the church. In the valleys of uncertainty, Paul seems to be almost spiritually broken, but then he was rebuilt in the strength of Spirit's power. He learned to depend not on his own personal qualities but on the greatness of almighty God. In the middle of his personal struggles with the false teachers at Corinth, he continuously seeks the spiritual well-being of the congregation. He wants them to succeed spiritually. Paul also realizes that for success to occur, the gospel must be defined. The false teachers at Corinth have denounced Paul and claimed that he is not a credible apostle and proclaimer of the gospel (2 Cor. 10–12). Paul knows he must rely solely on the wisdom of God and define the true gospel accordingly.

In addition, Paul is surrounded by trusted companions who share responsibility for defending the gospel at Corinth. When he entrusted others with leadership, he enabled his co-workers to help him in making positive and God-honoring decisions. The restoration of a divided congregation is never the sole duty of any one person. It is the responsibility of the entire body of Christ in cooperation with the Holy Spirit.

In the Corinthian crisis, God called people such as Paul, Timothy, Sosthenes, Titus, Apollos, Stephanas, Fortunatus, Achaicus, Aquila, Prisca, and others to the front lines to help define and defend a pure gospel (1 Cor. 1:1; 16:10-20). In the heat of battles to defend the faith, the wisdom of certain leaders stands out. Paul is such a person! Yet we cannot overestimate the importance of this cohesive group to Paul and the need for true Christian unity.

Congregation B divided over doctrinal reasons. The pastor no longer held to the doctrine of the denomination. After a new pastor was called, someone interviewed a former member of the congregation, who expressed hostility and unwillingness to return to the church. He had trusted and loved his pastor. He did not understand why the congregation did not want to follow him. He thought it was enough that his pastor had believed what he taught!

The congregation's leaders had attempted to restore order to the church. When the (former) pastor was dismissed, the hurt was felt in many lives. Eighty percent of the congregation quit attending the church. From all human perspectives, the church was nearly destroyed. Restoring congregational cohesiveness would take several years to accomplish, starting with the remaining membership. The seriousness of the problem seemed overwhelming to the few who remained faithful to the now-tiny congregation.

Whenever a church leader becomes the focus of serious contention, there will be people torn apart both spiritually and emotionally. The apostle Paul was accused of preaching wrong doctrines at Corinth. The accusations against him included pride, boasting, indecisiveness, physical weakness, rudeness in speech, ungifted preaching, dishonesty, foolishness, false apostolic standing, deception, being a charlatan, and denying the gospel's power. The false teachers at Corinth had every intention of making Paul their example and scapegoat.

Paul's defense of the gospel employs a method different from his accusers. He calls the church to holy living and declares himself to be an apostle of credibility, commissioned by the Lord himself (2 Cor. 10). Paul was in a leadership position where he could have ripped the heart out of the remaining cohesivenesss in the church by how he defended himself and attacked his opponents. How church leaders reply to their opponents is critically important in conflict resolution.

In congregation B (mentioned above), an additional sorrow was experienced over that unrestored pastor who will never again be allowed to preach in the denomination. When he denounced the doctrine of the church, he forfeited his ministerial credentials. Ethics should have dictated that pastor's direction. If he could no longer agree with the denominational position, he should have quietly resigned and left the church. His actions harmed many people. When a pastor signs his name, agreeing to support the denominational beliefs, he makes a promise.

All too often people justify their actions by how they feel now, and not by what they promised to do. There is a crisis of integrity among many clergy today. The apostle Paul confronted a similar problem, but from a different angle. He was faced with false apostles, newcomers in the church who were attempting to impose beliefs on members that were contrary to what Paul had taught. Paul had founded the church at Corinth. He faced an uphill battle to remove the influence of these false leaders. Paul faced many overwhelming circumstances before he would be able to present to God a glorious and reconciled congregation.

The need for effective restoration of divided congregations is mandatory if the effectiveness of the gospel is to be enhanced in local church areas. If the gospel is the gospel of love, then the church needs to communicate restoring love. This restoring love must be as equally true for the laypeople as it is for the pastor. One pastor adds, "We should never apologize for surgery when surgery is needed. When a band has someone out of tune, they remove the discord so harmony can exist."

In the church we are compelled by the love of Christ to teach and demonstrate the harmony of Christ. In so doing, we must remain true to the standards for our lives as transformed by Christ. Restoration involves the attempts of God's people to bring cohesiveness to the body of Christ. When necessary, it also involves the removal of cancerous material that can destroy the life of the body. The false teachers at Corinth were a cancer in the church. Strong medicine or surgery was needed.

We need to pray with fear and trembling as we decide what direction to proceed in a crisis to restore cohesiveness. The character of disunity is evil, and any attempt to restore the church body must be based on spiritual principles. Human souls and their fate in eternity are matters of great concern in restoration. The apostle Paul avoided any tactics other than proclaiming that the Corinthians urgently needed to separate themselves from all worldly attitudes and actions (2 Cor. 6:14—7:1).

More problems could be reviewed here. One might try to maintain that the church in crisis is just like any other human institution in the world. However, in the midst of conflict and tension, there are at least three divine truths in full operation in the church. These truths include the activity of God's grace, the necessity of worship, and the role of peacemaking. These truths always cooperate as forces used by God to destroy animosity between church factions in conflict with each other. The church in Corinth will be our primary example of these truths in operation.

The Work of Grace in the Letters to Corinth
Grace Active in the Church and in Paul's Ministry

Paul's concept of grace shown in the Corinthian letters presents a model for developing procedure to implement conflict resolution. The basic assumption of the paradigm is that both in the periods of congregational unity and disunity, the will of God remains unchanging. With our best human intuitions and reflections, we may perceive that the church is being destroyed by conflict. We must trust that the grace of God is already undertaking to restore the unity of the church. Since Christ is the head of the church, we must also conclude that he will always have every believer's best interest close to his heart.

The understanding of how Paul uses the word *grace* in the Corinthian letters is important for understanding this truth. First, in the salutations of both letters to the Corinthians, Paul changes the standard letter formula of the ancient world to incorporate a direct and revealing Christian message (1 Cor. 1:1-3; 2 Cor. 1:2). In ancient Hellenistic letters, the customary Greek word used for "greetings" was *chairein*. Paul chooses to use the related word *charis* (grace) with the Hebrew word *shalom* (peace). The bonding of these two terms reveals that God's favor in grace is the basis of our peace.

The Christian community is not obtained by human strength. Instead, it is achieved by the grace of God. In other words, we can labor hard in our attempts to reconcile a congregation in crisis. Our labor will be in vain unless we are willing to cooperate with the grace that is at work in us. Grace will accomplish peace in our lives. The Christian community has been formed by a bonding of both Jewish and Gentile believers in Christ's gospel (1 Cor. 1:2; 2 Cor. 1:1-2). Paul is vitally concerned that this bonding continually takes place in the context of his ministry. This is the cement of biblical fellowship. Those who once were estranged from each other, God has now made into brothers and sisters who love each other.

The true gospel of Christ demands a church which has been

bonded together on the strength of God's grace. Prejudices of the past which have separated people from each other are to be extinguished as members are united into one unified body. Paul intends his salutations to direct the Corinthians away from influences of false teachings in the congregation, and from their own sinful actions, reactions, and divisions. They are to be united in the Lord, who has placed the apostolic calling upon Paul's life. His defense of his apostolic calling is not based on human credentials. It is founded on a decision of God for his life. Paul's ministry to the Corinthians stands upon the grace of God, and so does their validity as a congregation.

Paul is an apostle by the will of God. He is fully convinced that his ministry is directed by God's will. Pastors and laypeople need to acquire the same type of attitude that the apostle Paul had. We must refuse to be ruled by misconceptions of our own self-importance on one hand, or of our commissioning from God on the other hand. If servants of Christ are truly to be peacemakers, they must depend upon God and his sovereignty in all of life. There are no immediate references to congregational problems as Paul greets his readers in 1 Corinthians. Yet we must conclude that the salutations themselves begin the apostle's defense of his calling to be the apostle of the church.

In addition to the involvement of grace in his apostolic calling, Paul concludes both these letters using the word *grace* (1 Cor. 16:23; 2 Cor. 13:13). Paul's usage of *grace* both in the salutations and in the conclusions of the Corinthian letters shows that grace is a central theme in Paul's message and strategy at Corinth. His formation of a methodology based on grace arises out of firm belief that God will not forsake his church when times are rough.

God is in the midst of our human battles to resolve conflict. After all, God's Son personally endured a cross to reconcile sinful men. Conflict resolution is dependent not only upon the grace of God, but also upon the human demonstration of divine love. In the church, our generation may be too quick to endorse

checklist strategies to resolve our conflicts and build our churches. We need to emphasize the spiritual method taught in the
Scriptures. The spiritual formula for conflict resolution is the im-
plementation of God's grace in the lives of each member of a
congregation.

I questioned eighty pastors about what they would do if they
were commissioned to serve a church in division. Many said that
in their pastoral experience, it would seem good for them to devise some type of methodology with which to resolve the conflict. Some said that they would deepen their commitment to
their prayer life. The example provided by Paul declares both
our need to depend upon the grace of God and our need to express divine love toward others in a personal way. Methodology
is important, but it must be based on spiritual formation if we expect it to resolve conflict in the church. The combination of these
two ingredients should prove to be a powerful tool in conflict
resolution.

Our concept of grace determines our enthusiasm for the
hard work of resolving conflict. Our understanding of grace at
work in the church provides a biblical hope in our labors; the
Lord says that when we have been taxed to our limit, God is still
at work.

The Corinthian letters declare grace in a second way: grace
has radically changed Paul's life. Grace has provided the only
recognizable stimulus for him to proclaim the gospel. We also
have been recipients of love, and that love gives energy in our
lives to press onward despite daily circumstances and their crip-
pling effect upon us. The apostle Paul states, "By the grace of
God I am what I am, and his grace toward me has not been in
vain. On the contrary, I worked harder than any of them—
though it was not I, but the grace of God that is with me" (1 Cor.
15:10).

God's grace changed Paul and gave him a place in the new
creation. He was made into an ambassador of the message of
reconciliation (2 Cor. 5:17-20). There is a primary difference be-

tween Paul's proclamation of the gospel and the gospel of the false apostles: Paul has experienced godly change in his own life, but they are peddling the word of God (2 Cor. 2:17). Paul's opponents are peddlers of a gospel that is foreign to the gospel of Christ. Their gospel does not demonstrate the lifestyle of following Jesus Christ. Paul's gospel does!

This concept of how Paul perceives grace is also found in 1 Corinthians, where he says, "According to the grace of God given to me, like a skilled master builder I laid a foundation" (1 Cor. 3:10). Grace enables Paul to proclaim the gospel of Jesus Christ and to carry out his apostolic assignment. Paul's faithfulness to the gospel is the product of grace. In his personal trials, he relates how God's grace has enabled him to stand fast in the ministry of reconciliation.

In 2 Corinthians Paul says, "Everything is for your sake, so that grace, as it extends to more and more people, may increase thanksgiving, to the glory of God" (2 Cor. 4:15). Paul's entire ministry is dependent upon grace. His experience with grace has produced a loving and humble attitude concerning life and ministry.

The idea that a spiritual congregation could be created apart from an action of grace is ludicrous. Many pastors have heard unhappy church members say things like this: "Those people in the church are the real troublemakers around here." There are no second-class citizens in the kingdom of God. All believers, whether we agree with them or not during times of crises and conflict, are called into grace. If this be so, and it is, then it is equally true that grace is at work, and we must let God perform his perfect will. All too often the need for change of heart is not so much in "those people" as in us.

Spiritual emancipation occurs when we let grace transform us into the character of Christ. In all our human strengths, we cannot change anyone who doesn't want change. The grace of God searches persistently for people who are willing to be changed into the image of Christ. This can only mean that we must acquire an abundant love for "those people." Such love will surely change the church!

Jesus said, "Why do you see the speck in your neighbor's eye, but do not notice the log in your own eye? Or how can you say to your neighbor, 'Let me take the speck out of your eye,' while the log is in your own eye?" (Matt. 7:3-4). The speck in our neighbor's eye is a shameful irritation that keeps him from seeing clearly. It is good to help the other person. We all need help from brothers and sisters. But how can we help others if a gigantic log is lodged in our own eye? Our vision about others is often wrong. Someone else may be wrong, and we may be wrong too.

Like all others, we have been contaminated by the sin of this fallen world in rebellion against God. The depth of our relationship to God depends upon our relationship with others. No matter how small a barrier others have between them and God, it is still a barrier. Honesty and integrity demand honest evaluations of situations.

However, we first need to know the truth about ourselves and see ourselves as we really are, without a system of phony excuses to hide behind. Then we would see that the log in our eye is monstrous in size. We would find it blinding and distasteful to all we hold dear and good in life. God is an all-revealing God. Grace searches the souls of all people. God will show us who we really are in the light of his Son's love. It is a unique individual who allows one's own self to be vulnerable by making one's true self and struggles known.

Grace deals with whole persons, teaching them holy dependence upon God. We don't want others to see our logs, but unless we become radically truthful, we will remain blinded. God wants us to develop holy dependence upon him. That will happen only when we are broken enough to open our lives up to the love of Christ and his examination. In brokenness, truth will find avenues to emerge in our lives. When we see our true self in light of Christ's love, we will discover that only through his love can we accomplish anything good in our lives. Success is measured by his standards and not our own. We find a joyous desire to please God and treat our fellow members as God would treat them.

Spiritual brokenness is the divinely appointed means toward freedom from all our fears. It is the first step for us to reconcile others to Christ. A congregation of members that will recognize their brokenness before God will be healed of division. In such places, the abundant grace of God is forever transforming willing participants to reflect God's love. Love demands change, and when congregations take seriously the love of God, then dissension and antagonism will flee. Paul was a man captured by love. In fact, he was in so much love for his Savior that he became his bond-servant. He willingly became a broken man to receive Christ's greater riches (cf. Heb. 11:24-26). Church restoration begins in grace, leads to love, and develops into joyous servanthood.

The Corinthians are in danger of vainly receiving the gospel by losing their hope in the grace of God as demonstrated in the resurrection. There are some at Corinth who believe strongly in the resurrection. Paul realizes that the grace demonstrated through the resurrection will be evident in the future bodily resurrection of believers. He rests upon this hope to help bring partial peace into the church. He is broken, and yet he is hopeful that what God has begun in the church will bear fruit. He is a man gladly willing to live contrary to the world's system of sanity, so he can be used by the wisdom of God (2 Cor. 4:1-12).

Paul desires that grace not be received in vain. He wants grace to touch all of his life. Grace has turned him around. It is no small matter for him to be part of the new creation in Christ. The very thought of being made new is revolutionary, the most radical thought Paul knows. God has reconciled us in order to give us the ministry of reconciliation. He has given us newness of life (2 Cor. 5:17-21; Rom. 6:4-5). Paul says, "This is our boast, the testimony of our conscience: we have behaved in the world with frankness and godly sincerity, not by earthly wisdom but by the grace of God—and all the more toward you" (2 Cor. 1:12).

Paul is concerned to establish godly integrity among the Corinthians. He knows that for this to occur, God will need to supply an act of grace and have the Spirit actively intercede for the believers at Corinth. Paul believes that this is already occurring in their lives, even though he may not yet be able to see the final results.

Many in our congregations are afraid to let our lives be examined by others, but believers with integrity have risked this. Such believers have nothing to fear and nothing to hide because they live the standard of love. They have died to selfish causes and seek to be approved by God. Paul says, "Examine yourselves to see whether you are living in the faith" (2 Cor. 13:5; 1 Cor. 11:28). The work of grace must be established in the life and ministry of the servants of God. Just as the definition of the gospel is at stake in the Corinthian church, so also its integrity must be demonstrated by the actions and reactions in the congregation's daily lifestyles.

Paul in his proclamation of the gospel also declares that God has manifested his grace in Paul's own life as God faithfully rescued him in trials. Paul soberly awaits the day of the bodily resurrection. But as he waits, he also experiences many types of trials. He longs to be with the Lord; at the same time, he struggles with the need to stay on earth. This is for the benefit of the church (2 Cor. 5:6-11).

Paul's opponents do not think his faith and work are worthy of honor. His stubbornness of faith leads him to the purifying waters of suffering. He waits in hope of Christ's deliverance from all things. One of the hardest things for the most noble of saints to do is to wait on God to move and give direction. We often fail because we attempt God's work through our own strength rather than by the movement of the Spirit. Those who would be the sons of God must be led by the Spirit.

In 2 Corinthians, Paul speaks of the hardships endured by him in Asia: "We do not want you to be unaware, brothers and sisters, of the affliction we experienced in Asia; for we were so utterly, unbearably crushed that we despaired of life itself. Indeed, we felt that we had received the sentence of death so that we would rely not on ourselves but on God who raises the dead. He who rescued us from so deadly a peril will continue to rescue us; on him we have set our hope that he will rescue us again" (2 Cor. 1:8-10).

In this suffering at Ephesus for the gospel, Paul centers his attention on the resurrection of the dead and God's ability to deliver from the perils of death. His hope is intact and growing. Grace will keep him no matter what may be thrown at him. Paul had developed a confidence in God's grace not only to deliver him but also to care for him through hardship (2 Cor. 1:12). Paul was referring to a past event in Asia. Though it was still fresh in his mind, he has been led to faithfully trust in the sufficient grace of God.

Paul writes, "God is able to provide you with every blessing in abundance, so that by always having enough of everything, you may share abundantly in every good work" (2 Cor. 9:8). In this passage, Paul is concerned about the offering for the needy saints in Jerusalem. He reminds the Corinthians of the generosity of the poverty-stricken Macedonians and how God has blessed them in giving beyond their ability. The Corinthians as well as the Macedonians need to understand that God is willing and able to help his church care for fellow members in the body of Christ. The Macedonian Christians are bonded together in their devotion to the Lord. They have given themselves first to the Lord, and then also to co-ministry with Paul (8:5). Consequently, God's loving grace is their reward.

In the midst of crisis, congregations often face a drop in financial contributions to the church. Here Paul provides a possible remedy for the problem. Generosity begets generosity. Grace begets grace even in the midst of church dissension. Paul appeals to the Corinthians to be gracious. Their graciousness should reflect the grace they have received from the Lord. "You know the generous act of our Lord Jesus Christ, that though he was rich, yet for your sakes he became poor, so that by his poverty you might become rich" (2 Cor. 8:9). Paul reminds them that God will graciously care for their every need when in responsible stewardship they serve him. God does not promise great riches, only merciful compassion for those who will identify with him.

Paul is thankful for the sufficiency of grace in the struggles of life. He has prayerfully requested that God remove the thorn in his flesh that has troubled him excessively. God has refused. There is much debate over what the problem was. Paul accepted God's answer to his prayer: "My grace is sufficient for you, for [my] power is made perfect in weakness." Paul says, "I will boast all the more gladly of my weaknesses, so that the power of Christ may dwell in me" (2 Cor. 12:9).

Paul must depend upon grace to live and defend the gospel of Jesus Christ. He cannot depend upon some ecstatic revelation to give him superiority over his enemies. He cannot depend upon his apostolic office to give him credibility. He cannot depend upon his intellect. He cannot depend on others to solve all his problems. His defense of the gospel is undertaken in the grace of God. He must rely exclusively on the power of Christ. There is no substitute for this in the church. The Holy Spirit is the administrator of all the ministries of the church. The Spirit alone is able to restore the church.

Grace at Corinth and in the Church Today

It is far easier to view crisis in the church as a permanent problem rather than as a temporary concern of the church. Each year some congregations must close their doors due to division; yet grace is always working in the lives of God's people. Christ is the head of the church. Hence, in every crisis, we can have assurance that Christ has determined to guide every believer and congregation through the turmoil and unto the perfecting of holiness (2 Cor. 7:1). God has immense patience and wisdom to lead his people through any encounter with evil. He is determined that his church will arise as victors in the battles against sin.

Church attenders often endanger themselves by insisting that they need to escape the problems of the church by leaving rather than addressing what originally caused the problems. They violate the biblical imperative of gathering for worship in humbleness before God and among fellow members (Heb. 10:25). Sometimes they leave for another congregation to avoid tension. Again, in every church crisis, grace is working in behalf of every believer.

In the operation of grace, God is concerned that each believer bear more and better fruit. That means pruning for our lives and for our churches (John 15:2). Pruning can hurt when our pride and stubbornness stand between us and God's peace. Through grace, Christ's love is continuously being manifested as we are being disciplined by the Lord to live in holiness. Without the intervention of such grace, the church would die. It would be like a spiritual jellyfish, having no backbone to conquer the problems of life.

In church B, unity and love within the congregation was eventually restored. The church had experienced a tragic downturn in attendance. After the congregation had endured many months of struggle, they discovered the grace of God. One leader in consensus with others said, "We have been pruned back. Watch out, world, we are going to grow!" The blessing for this believer caught in the church conflict was discovered when he realized that the trials of grace were worked out by Christ's perfect will. When they understood this, the believer and the congregation were both strengthened in their walks with the Lord.

The above-mentioned leader was excited because he had discovered that God's grace was still operating in the life of the congregation. From a human point of view, the problems had seemed to be impossible to overcome. But in those months of turmoil, God had not turned his back on the remnant of the congregation that remained after the crisis. God has never promised that rebuilding would be easy. One person said it this way: "God expects us to do what is possible. He will do the impossible."

The love of God for his church never ceases. A year prior, the former pastor had been fired because of doctrinal differences with the congregation; he declared the church would be dead by the end of the summer. Many people had quit attending. It didn't die. Through God's grace and the efforts of peacemaking, it began to grow. Some congregations do die. The will of God for the church is not death, but life. God calls the church into existence to be the light and salt of the earth. In dealing with congregations in crisis, denominational leaders should be careful not to interfere with the action of grace that God is performing within the church. It is a solemn thing to close the doors of a church.

Congregational Worship in the Corinthian Letters

To establish an environment conducive for conflict resolution among the Corinthians, the apostle Paul needed to establish a consistent standard of worship. Throughout the many centuries of Christianity, there have been many definitions of worship. The following is one attempt toward understanding the importance of worship in the context of conflict resolution. Worship is the establishment and maintenance of holy living through Jesus Christ, both corporately by the body of Christ gathered together, and individually by the believer in Christ. Worship is more than a planned program or service. It is a way of life.

The church is divinely appointed to receive God's grace. The strategic mission of proclaiming the love of Christ to all peoples cannot be accomplished with a watered-down and polluted gospel. The apostle understood that worship must seriously undertake conformity to a consistent lifestyle of holiness as declared in the Scriptures. The apostle Paul in 2 Corinthians 6:14—7:1 urges the Corinthians to cleanse themselves from all defilement of the flesh and the spirit. He informs them that they must perfect holiness in the fear of God. The mission of proclamation demands Christian purity.

The church is to worship God not only in the formal gatherings of the members, but also in everything that the individual believer engages in during daily life. Hence, worship becomes more than just a Sunday morning exercise in religion. It involves total and undivided allegiance to God in every part of our daily living. Christianity must strongly endorse worship involving a communion with God that allows all of life to be an exercise in worship. Paul continually encourages total conformity to this standard of life. It is not enough to define worship only in the context of Christians assembling together in a formal service. This disregards the character of worship as encompassing all of life. We should meditate on God's will day and night (Ps. 1:2) and "do everything for the glory of God" (1 Cor. 10:31).

A number of parameters regarding worship flow through the Corinthian letters. With these themes, Paul attempts to reconcile the church in love for one another and for Christ.

Worship Related to Cross and Resurrection

The resurrection is the focus of all joyous fellowship and worship. Through this divine act, God declares that Jesus Christ not only paid the penalty of humanity's sins, but also that God has proven his sovereign right to forgive. He declares that Christ is the firstfruits of many resurrections yet to come (1 Cor. 15:20). This is the focal point of all joyous worship. The grave has lost its victory and sting.

The events of the cross and the resurrection have set in motion millions of spiritual events declaring that the kingdom of God is powerfully impacting lives. The outpouring of divine love is occurring everywhere (2 Cor. 4:15). People's lives are being transformed so that they become holy participants of love. There can be no experience of such wondrous streams of love apart from the hope of Christ's resurrection and his promise of many resurrections. This thought and hope impact human hearts to such a degree that a revolution is occurring. People can now boldly turn their allegiance away from everything that is in conflict with the kingdom of God.

The outcome for our lives is an understanding of what joy we have been granted by God. True worship is endowed with true joy. Worship is a celebration of grace provided for us by God himself. The cousin of such celebration is reverence toward God. This encourages the Christian to participate in the holy standards of the kingdom of God. Where there is joy in worship, there is also spiritual renewal and love.

All Christian congregations should firmly understand that they must worship in a world hostile to the love of Christ. Jesus Christ is the model for believers to follow in their own lives. Paul's ministry reflected this attitude: "We are God's servants, working together; you are God's field, God's building. According to the grace of God given to me, like a skilled master builder I laid a foundation, and someone else is building on it. Each builder must choose with care how to build on it. For no one can lay any foundation other than the one that has been laid; that foundation is Jesus Christ" (1 Cor. 3:9-11).

Paul has modeled this crucial foundation of worship for the church. His opponents at Corinth are charging that his ministry is deceitful. For Paul, ministry and worship go hand in hand. Paul forces them to prove him wrong by God's standard of worship. He responds by neither compromising the gospel nor his integrity: "Give no offense to Jews or to Greeks or to the church of God, just as I try to please everyone in everything I do, not seeking my own advantage, but that of many, so that they may be saved. Be imitators of me, as I am of Christ" (1 Cor. 10:32—11:1).

The church has received resurrection power and is God's earthly dwelling place. This means that every member needs to participate individually and corporately in obedient worship. Paul's imitation of Christ is his worship. He imitates Christ in all circumstances of life. No matter what may happen in life, there is room for worship. Paul lives a life of worship. He practices the presence of God. Worship to him is life. He wants the Corinthians to worship too. He wants them to see him as a servant of God (1 Cor. 4:1-17).

Paul speaks further about his leadership ministry:

> We are putting no obstacle in anyone's way, so that no fault may be found with our ministry, but as servants of God we have commended ourselves in every way: through great endurance, in afflictions, hardships, calamities, beatings, imprisonments, riots, labors, sleepless nights, hunger; by purity, knowledge, patience, kindness, holiness of spirit, genuine love, truthful speech, and the power of God; with the weapons of righteousness for the right hand and for the left; in honor and dishonor, in ill repute and good repute. We are treated as impostors, and yet are true; as unknown, and yet are well known; as dying, and see—we are alive; as punished, and yet not killed; as sorrowful, yet always rejoicing; as poor, yet making many rich; as having nothing, and yet possessing everything. (2 Cor. 6:3-10)

Paul is aware that how he responds to the criticisms of his opponents will determine the fate of many believers in their quest to consistently worship God. He chooses to be a reflection of God's glory; he desires no human praise. Paul realizes that defining the parameters of the gospel is at stake. The very warp and woof of the gospel is the resurrection. The resurrection provides the motivation to worship. In Paul's human weakness, he desires that God would be glorified.

Paul's lifestyle is proof that he practices what he preaches. Let the Corinthian opponents judge him according to his possession of holy character. That should be our attitudes toward ministers of the gospel, too! The Corinthians, rather than being allowed to choose sides concerning Paul, are hit between the eyes with the choice of whether or not they will worship undefiled before God. To do this means they must admit that their human weaknesses and passions have competed with the goal of perfecting holiness in the fear of God. The tension that exists at Corinth is not rooted in Paul's human weaknesses. It is spiritual opposition conceived in human rebellion toward God. This rebellion is targeted against true spiritual worship.

True spiritual worship is light to the souls of people. True spiritual worship will shatter the darkness of minds depraved by sin. True spiritual worship is the greatest threat to the kingdom of Satan and his lies. The cross and the resurrection are intended by God to set people free by a new life and hope in Christ. Worship based on this becomes the supreme standard of life. If the church is united together in celebration of Christ's victory over sin and death, it discovers the reason for its existence. Believers exist by the grace of God, to worship joyously and truthfully. Satan's strategy is to attack the character of the church by destroying its worship. Where there is no worship, the church will no longer exist in that place.

Worship Related to Spiritual Wisdom

The resolution of conflict in the church begins with the recognition that in conflict, sinful responses have occurred. These sinful responses are counterproductive to worship. Paul writes, "So, brothers and sisters, I could not speak to you as spiritual people, but rather as people of the flesh, as infants in Christ" (1 Cor. 3:1). In Corinth, some church people are living as if they have never experienced the grace of God. Their fleshly lives have produced conflict in the church. Their carnality has robbed them of spiritual maturity. Paul's opponents are destroying the congregation's unity. They are now possessed with jealousy and strife. They are living like the carnal world. One could see little difference between how his opponents are living and how unbelievers live.

Paul's antidote is for them to become possessors of the Spirit's wisdom and power. As he writes his letters, he realizes that he must address both the spiritual and the carnal at Corinth.

He reminds them that he does not come to them with superior wisdom. In fact, he places no weight on his wisdom to announce the testimony of God, yet he continues to proclaim it. He is interested in one main item in his ministry. He must preach Jesus Christ and him crucified. To enhance this concept, he says, "My speech and my proclamation were not with plausible words of wisdom, but with a demonstration of the Spirit and of power" (1 Cor. 2:4). The Holy Spirit is manifested in Paul's life and behavior. He is living by the grace of God rather than by earthly wisdom (2 Cor. 1:12).

In Paul's life, ministry is centered around the proclamation of the death, burial, and resurrection of the Lord. The Spirit has been constantly interacting with the Corinthian church ever since the first person there believed on Christ. They do not owe their origin to human wisdom. The wisdom of the resurrection is not of this age, yet its power changes lives by transforming them into Christlikeness. The role of the Spirit of God is to reveal the cross by implanting within believers spiritual wisdom concerning its meaning to sinful people.

Paul informs the Corinthians that they have not received the spirit of the world, but the Spirit of God (1 Cor. 2:12; chaps. 12–13). The Spirit has been given to people that they might know the things God has given to them. The Holy Spirit teaches believers both spiritual thoughts and words about the truth of Christ. The Spirit is the Counselor of all counselors, able to interpret all actions, thoughts, beliefs, and lives of people.

Spiritual wisdom is a gift of God. God gives spiritual wisdom to his people to enable them to stand against the darkened foolishness of the world. The Christians' spiritual wisdom allows them to recognize that life has value beyond life in this world. They worship because they are committed to the kingdom of God and the lordship of Christ over their life. Their life has found joy not in the values of a world in rebellion against God, but rather in Christ himself. The Christians' life and lifestyle are reflections of their commitment to the authority of Jesus Christ.

Paul addresses carnal believers who live as though life were just eat, drink, and be merry, for tomorrow we die (1 Cor. 3:1; 15:32). What a shame to live as if life is finalized at death! The greatness of God is that God loves us and has given eternal life to those who repent. Joy in worship is the expression of human emotions in thanks for God's love and grace.

Spiritual things can only be understood by a person who is the possession of the Holy Spirit. The Holy Spirit is the only vehicle God has provided to give people the understanding of the love of God. The Spirit alone provides true spiritual wisdom (1 Cor. 2).

The fleshly people in the church at Corinth are spiritual infants in their understanding of spiritual things. They have not grown in their spiritual lives. They are living with the wisdom of the world as they try to conduct the business of the church. How sad it is to pretend to be something when one can't even begin to measure up! It is as if the spiritually blind are trying to lead the ones who are seeing the reality of the kingdom of God in their lives.

The word Paul uses to describe these "people of the flesh" applies to those who remain in corruption and are imperfectly acquainted with the church (1 Cor. 3:1-5). They only know the world's wisdom, which is seriously limited. Paul has been forced to feed them with spiritual milk. They are so deprived that they cannot digest a solid diet of spiritual nutrition. He would rather give them spiritual meat, but they are unable to understand it at the present time. He continues to feed them so that they may discover the importance of Jesus Christ and him crucified.

Not all believers are spiritually mature in Christ. The opponents of Paul were the enemies of the cross. The fleshly believers at Corinth were the victims of their deception. Yet they were held responsible for not growing up into maturity. The overwhelming problem at Corinth is not just a difference of opinions among believers. The problem is tension between spiritual persons and fleshly persons. Therefore, Paul demands that they maintain or reclaim spiritual cohesiveness. This is one of the parameters of true spiritual worship.

Worship Related to Spiritual Cohesiveness

Spiritual wisdom must be the companion of the believer's entire life. When a congregation is divided, it should recognize that the negative reactions of people represent a barometer. That barometer reflects the overall spiritual health of the congregation in addressing its relationship to Jesus Christ. Worship entails a spiritual intimacy and cohesiveness with God. This relationship bonds each member of the body of Christ together (1 Cor. 12:12-27).

Worship is grounded in the love of Christ. It is exhibited in human life through relating to the sufferings of Christ and praising God despite suffering hostilities of the moment. The resolution of conflict at Corinth carries no promises of a speedy solution. In fact, there is no supportive evidence that the conflicts at Corinth were ever resolved. History records that problems either continued into the next generation or were periodically revived in the Corinthian house churches. Paul repeatedly pleads for all division to cease and for cohesiveness to be restored (1 Cor. 1:10; 3:3; 11:18; 2 Cor. 13:10-13).

History is full of examples of conflicts in the church. One of the most touching appeals came from the emperor Constantine. He called the first empire-wide church conference to stop the Arian heresy. In his opening statement to three hundred bishops, he said,

> I must thank God that, in addition to all the other blessings, he has shown me this highest one of all: to see you all gathered here in harmony and with one mind. . . . Discord in the church I consider more fearful and painful than any other war. As soon as I, by the help of God, had overcome my enemies, I believed that nothing more was now necessary than to give thanks to God in common joy with those whom I had liberated. But when I heard of your division, I was

convinced that this matter should by no means be neglected, and in the desire to assist by my service, I have summoned you without delay. . . . My friends, delay not. . . . Put away all causes of strife, and loose all knots of discord by the laws of peace. Thus you shall accomplish the works most pleasing to God, and confer upon me, your fellow servant, an exceedingly great joy. (Christian History Institute's "Glimpses," issue 65)

All generations of the church have experienced troubles both from within and from without. Our generation will experience them, too. This is a fallen world in rebellion against God. A congregation that attempts to exist on a corner in suburbia and thus to hide from any type of trouble will likely find itself stagnant. Conflict is our enemy, and yet it is a great purifier of life.

Conflict resolution becomes even more urgent when we see that the lack of church cohesiveness is related to the kingdom of God being in tension with the kingdom of darkness. Satan's kingdom of darkness is always promoting its agenda to destroy the worship of the church. If we let that darkness stifle the message of reconciliation through the cross and the joyous praise for what God has done, then the church will die spiritually.

Paul, however, promotes a redeeming gospel. He also acknowledges that the gospel is veiled to those who are perishing (2 Cor. 4:3). With a humble attitude, he declares that the treasure of heaven has been given to clay jars such as himself (4:7). The proclamation of the gospel has been given to weak human beings (the church) to communicate to the peoples of the world. When the church recognizes its weaknesses, it is supplied graciously through faith to do what is humanly impossible to accomplish. The proclamation becomes an act of worship. The church is not called to engage itself in war against its own members. Paul requires his congregation to model his actions and stewardship before God. It is often difficult for believers to acknowledge that they have done wrongful acts that can only be considered evil. Repentance is needed even within the church.

The work of restoration at Corinth demands that the church must exist within the parameters of true worship. They must recognize where sin has crept into their lives. They must repent of all sin. They must receive the apostle's discipline as from the Lord. There must be forgiveness without compromising the essence of the gospel. Paul writes concerning one who has sinned and repented, "This punishment by the majority is enough for such a person; so now instead you should forgive and console him, so that he may not be overwhelmed by excessive sorrow" (2 Cor. 2:6-7).

Not only does Paul cast spiritual judgment; also, in the integrity of each believer's worship, he calls them into serious questioning of their own sins. The entire congregation is to become involved with the discipline and restoration of the individual. The entire church is accountable to preserve congregational cohesiveness and worship.

Human ability to worship is affected if we yield to evil. To promote restoration from sin and to enhance the ability to worship, we must discover the spiritual issues present. Paul in 1 Corinthians engages in dialogue over particular issues occurring at Corinth such as incest, meat offered to idols, conduct in worship services, and so forth. The apostle realizes that the outward and revealed sins of the congregation are only the tip of the iceberg. There are underlying misunderstandings that must be dealt with if worship is to continue to perfect holiness in the fear of God. These misunderstandings involve the defining of what the gospel is and is not. Paul sees himself as being in partnership with the Corinthians. Worship always involves a partnership with God and among people.

In 1 Corinthians 14, Paul writes concerning problems appearing in worship services. The worship of the church has lost its ability to edify the participants. Confusion is prevalent in the congregation. The apostle orders changes in the worship format. The question that must be addressed is this: Is the worship failing to edify because of its format? Or is it failing because of a failure to distinguish between true worship on one hand, and human emotion and tradition on the other hand? The Corinthians were failing in worship because of their confusion over the believers' role as the temple of God (1 Cor. 3:16-17; 6:14-20) and their struggles with allegiance to the kingdom of God. Hence, the entire study of resolution at Corinth must take a spiritual perspective in conflict resolution.

The problem then becomes not so much a clash between human opponents as a tension between principles governing the kingdom of God and the satanic opposition to it. We are called to holy living. The answer to church conflict is discovering that worship is found in obedient life in Christ. Worship is not just a meeting of humans together on a Sunday morning. It is a continuous intimacy with God. As the Corinthians discover true worship and obedience in relationship to holiness, they will also discover congregational spiritual cohesiveness.

Peacemaking in Conflict Resolution

As Paul and his companions ponder the themes of worship and grace, they gain an increasing awareness of the need for peacemaking. The goals of peacemaking provide a unique opportunity to establish and demonstrate the lordship of Christ over each member of the body of Christ. Jesus said, "Blessed are the peacemakers, for they will be called children of God" (Matt. 5:9). The foundation upon which all biblical peacemaking efforts rest is in the understanding that God has made peace through the blood of the cross (Col. 1:20). This act of God is the only vehicle for all human reconciliation with God and peace among people.

First, the goal of peacemaking is not just the removal of conflict from our lives and from congregations. Much more, it is a summons to spiritual battle, strengthening in crisis, and emancipation from evil. Its goal is to conquer the debilitating tensions which cripple people, and to do this through a spiritual release by Christ. Peacemakers are to engage their faith against the kingdom of darkness (2 Cor. 4). They use holy weapons to love others and to destroy the consequences of sin lingering in human lives (2 Cor. 10:4). It is shameful when members direct anger, hatred, revenge, bitterness, and hostility against others in the family of God. Peacemaking seeks the advancement of friendship with each other through spiritual bonding with each other.

Peacemaking is hard work. It is complex because it demands the humanly impossible for all who are involved with conflict and its resolution. It demands the disarmament of the weapons of carnality by insisting that brothers and sisters love each other. The peacemaking process is never peaceful for those caught in the emotions of the conflict. Peacemakers are challenged to engage in both loving and peaceful cohesiveness with one another (John 13:34-35; 1 Cor. 10:24; 2 Cor. 13:11-13; Phil. 2:14; Rom. 15:2; Heb. 13:1-2; Prov. 15:33).

Second, the mandate of Scripture is for us to pursue peace with all people to the best of our abilities (Heb. 12:12-17; James 4:6-7; 5:19-20; Rom. 15:5; 12:12-17).

Third, if the peacemaking process fails, it does not mean that the Holy Spirit has failed. It does not necessarily mean that the peacemakers have failed. God is perfect and cannot fail (Matt. 5:48). Peacemakers, being fallible, may fail in their role of peacemaking. Those in conflict may refuse to be reconciled, too. To refuse to be reconciled is a problem related to sin (Matt. 6:14-15; Mark 11:22-26).

Many pastors and laypeople have beat themselves over the head for apparent failures in peacemaking. Peacemaking is God's undertaking. The Lord is the only one who knows how to deal with sinful hearts, the only one who knows how to produce peace. To the relief of the peacemaker, God is always working in the lives of people. Self-blame only makes sense when the peacemaker has knowingly caused further problems in conflict resolution by disobeying God. The human response toward peacemaking must be obedience to God (1 Sam. 15:22; Matt. 7:21; Exod. 19:5; Josh. 1:8).

Fourth, since nothing can separate us from the love of God, we can be assured that the Holy Spirit is always attempting to restore those who have fallen away from the Lord (John 16:7-15; Rom. 8:26-39). Whenever the Word of God is preached, God is seeking to reconcile people.

Fifth, since we have a mandate to be peacemakers, we must encourage those in conflict to be reconciled to God and the family of God. The importance of reconciliation for spiritual health cannot be overemphasized. Biblical reconciliation will pull out the root of bitterness and distrust that wrecks relationships.

The Pastoral Role in Peacemaking
Basic Pastoral Attitudes Toward Peacemaking

We need to deploy peacemaking strategy in congregations in crisis if a spiritual beachhead is to be established that will advance the mission of the church. Many pastors have shunned pastoral assignments to troubled congregations. This is sad because within the ministry of reconciliation, there are opportunities to experience the abundant grace and mercy of the Lord. Responsible pastoral leadership must develop special attitudes if peacemaking is to take place. Eighty pastors were asked what they would do if they were given a call to serve in a divided congregation. Some of these pastors had experienced a church in crisis. These pastors shared several important *guidelines:*

· 1. The pastoral peacemaker must create a safe climate in the church for honest exchange of feelings. The pastor must reduce the fear of different groups in the church, fear that they might be excluded. This can be done by examining all the perceived threats to the congregation's sense of community.

2. Pastoral peacemakers must learn personally the loving acceptance and forgiveness of God in one's own daily life. They must continually learn this if they are going to teach and practice it in the congregation. Ministry must be established through fairness and firmness toward all in the church. The pastoral peacemaker must plan to establish congregational direction toward

specific goals of cohesiveness.

3. The pastoral peacemaker must spend much time with appointed leadership. The pastor must continuously be involved in the healing of hurting leaders in the congregation. The pastor must demonstrate God's love by ministering to the entire church family, without showing favoritism.

4. The pastoral peacemaker must learn to live above the petty squabbles in the church. The pastor must be assertive in love and thus an example for the entire congregation. It is also important in this quest for the pastoral leader to keep oneself physically fit. This will help in keeping attitudes positive in times of tension.

5. The pastoral peacemaker must learn to listen with a prayerful attitude. The pastor must develop skill in perceiving when it is beneficial to move quickly in making changes, and when it is necessary to move slowly. Members in some churches will not be emotionally ready to advance in the mission of the church. The peacemaker must always listen before acting.

Developing these attitudes and patterns of action will advance conflict resolution. In addition, the pastoral peacemaker must also give attention to what is important to restoring cohesiveness in the congregation. Here are a number of *concerns:*

1. Establishing facts concerning the conflict, not just going by what some self-interested group is saying.

2. Establishing a disciplined prayer life, where intercession is made continuously for the church.

3. Seeking counsel from trusted denominational and local leadership. The peacemakers must be careful in choosing from whom they seek counsel.

The pastoral peacemaker needs to negotiate for the resolution of the conflict by the following *actions:*

1. Attempting to discern the causes of the conflict and dealing with them in integrity. The pastor should intercede with warring parties to seek reconciliation and forgiveness for any unloving attitudes or actions. The pastor needs to ask that appro-

priate repentance and restitution be made for unloving deeds. This should be done in accord with Matthew 18:15-20.

2. Being responsive to each believer, listening to the stories of conflict. The pastor must keep ears open to the hurts of the congregation.

3. Being willing to meet with those of differing opinions on a confidential level. Insist that confidences be respected. Be alert to danger when a clan shares among its number confidential information from others and uniformily echoes the family leader's opinion. As an antidote, urge each one to seek the mind of Christ (1 Cor. 2:16).

4. Promoting a positive pastoral image through preaching, personal contacts, and written items such as bulletins and newsletters. The pastor must always emphasize the positive benefits of working through the problems of the church. The pastor must proclaim a glorious gospel of reconciliation, love, and forgiveness.

5. Identifying common goals and tasks in order to move the congregation into creative and joyful Christianity. Some congregations will want to move too quickly while others will be frustrated when they discover failure due to unresolved problems from the past.

6. Concentrating on those who remain. The pastoral peacemaker will fail in some conflict resolution. When negotiating collapses and people leave the congregation permanently, it is necessary to concentrate one's efforts on those who remain in the congregation rather than exhausting oneself in chasing after those who have deserted the church of the living God. Some may return, but most won't. This is sad, yet it appears to be true.

7. Establishing a loving separation of the congregation from the former pastor when the source of tension has been over the pastoral office. The peacemaking pastor must be aware that in many church problems, the pastor will take the brunt of the people's attention and anger whether the pastor is or is not the person at fault. In restoring the church to unity, the peacemaker

must be careful not to use the previous pastor as a scapegoat, to bear all the blame. In some cases, it may be necessary to resolve conflict by involving the previous pastor in the negotiations. This is not always a good idea, but some situations may require it.

8. Developing congregational opportunities for fellowship and fun, formally and informally.

9. Giving the congregation time to adjust to new pastoral leadership, and to the new pastor's ways of showing love to them. The pastor must develop one's own leadership style, refusing to let that style be molded by the conflictive circumstances of the congregation.

10. Encouraging planning for the future. This is particularly difficult in times when the conflict has reached a peak.

11. Remaining true to the commitment the pastor made to the congregation when agreeing to become the pastor. If the pastor agreed to serve the church for a specific time period, that word must be lived out. Sometimes when the going gets difficult, there is a desire to bail out of the commitment. It is necessary to be sensible in our commitments to congregations. In some cases it may be better for the congregation and the pastor to agree to separate before a term is finished.

12. Visualizing one's pastoral call in terms of an interim assignment. Many congregations would be much wiser to have an interim pastor after severe crisis than trying to accommodate a long-term pastoral call. This allows for special focus on healing that may climax when a long-term pastor is called.

13. Remaining in agreement with the standards of the denomination. This is good pastoral ethics.

14. Feeling at ease with bringing to the church outside resource persons such as a Christian psychologist or counselor.

15. Stabilizing all church programs and evaluating their importance to the congregation.

16. Stopping gossip. The pastor must also be willing to receive criticism based on the principles of Matthew 18:15-20.

17. Helping people hear the other side of their concerns, and understanding their need to love those with whom they have disagreement.

18. Willing to spend many hours in prayer, Bible study, meetings, and visitation. The peacemaker can expect the help of God.

The role of the pastoral peacemaker is difficult and complex. When a congregation feels that it has been betrayed by the congregational membership, lay leaders, or their pastor, they discover that their ability to trust is lowered. Some or all of the preceding concerns will be addressed by the peacemaker who has been placed in a position where the motives of leadership are considered suspicious: lack of trust, lowered finances, relationships with the former pastor that are both positive and negative, depression, attitudes of anger and bitterness, family divisions, future participation of lay leaders in the business of the church, and church attendance.

The apostle Paul in his negotiations with the Corinthians may have used many of the suggestions mentioned above to restore cohesiveness in the church.

A Peacemaking Vision Among Leadership

"We have never done it this way before," said the old faithful member of the church. In church crisis it is necessary for the pastoral peacemaker to transcend the barrier between the maintenance mentality of ministry and to seek creative spiritual growth. It is easy in a church crisis to be caught like the little Dutch boy, maintaining the dike by keeping his finger in the hole and neglecting the larger problem.

At first, maintenance ministry may be necessary to allow for special nurturing essential for the church to continue to exist. However, sooner or later the peacemaker must direct the congregation from an attitude of maintenance into a consciousness of spiritual advancement. Jesus said, "Go therefore and make disciples of all nations, baptizing them in the name of the Father and of the Son and of the Holy Spirit, and teaching them to obey everything that I have commanded you. And remember, I am with you always, to the end of the age" (Matt. 28:19-20).

The command is to go and make disciples. This command does not change. It is still the peacemaker's role to wisely lead the congregation into growth at a pace that both nurtures and challenges the believer. Nongrowth attitudes do not change overnight. The attitudes that encourage dissension and crisis in a congregation do not normally disappear overnight. God is more interested in working in our lives than in sidestepping problems.

In cooperation with the laity, the pastoral peacemaker must secure the power to make necessary adjustments that will encourage growth. Growth will affect finances, spiritual maturity, congregational body-life, and evangelistic zeal. If a congregation in a depressed and turbulent stage is to acquire motivation to grow, it must have leadership that has been earned by both the pastoral position and by lay leadership. Functional authority is the power granted to leadership by virtue of the office of pastor. Acquired leadership authority is earned by the pastoral peacemaker while directing the congregation in conflict resolution. It is necessary for both types of authority to be granted to the pastoral peacemaker if the nongrowth mentality is to be conquered.

To allow a congregation to remain in the grip of their own status-quo mentality is unloving; it is yielding to what is dragging the congregation down, and it also declares that the congregation is stagnated. The apostle Paul declares to the Corinthians that they are babies being nurtured on spiritual milk. Some have regressed spiritually. They cannot digest the meat of an ongoing diet of spiritual growth. There must come a time in church restoration when peacemaking leaves the comfortable congregational pew to risk helping the membership to grow spiritually and numerically. Congregational disunity will destroy productivity in the church if allowed to go unchecked.

Sometimes it takes an encounter with a serious problem to shock people into action. For example, church B (mentioned above) had experienced three years of peacemaking efforts directed toward providing congregational restoration. There had been much concern about maintaining the church; the congregation was oriented toward meeting a minimum standard for existence rather than making any attempt to grow. The present congregation could not overcome the financial debt that had occurred both during and after the initial crisis. With the loss of people during the conflict, the income of the church was lowered disastrously.

Many suggestions were examined to find a solution for the finances of the church. Bills were piling up and seemed almost impossible to handle. The leaders jolted the congregation by suggesting four possible solutions to the problem of finances. They could close the church. They could release the full-time pastor and hire a part-time pastor. They could remain as they were and hope for the best. They could be taken over by another growth-oriented congregation as a special project for expansion.

In the final option, there was a risk that the other congregation would assume all decision making in the troubled congregation. They would model Christ's love for the congregation. The present congregational leaders would lose power to decide for themselves what the direction of the church would be in the future. Wisely, the church leadership realized their own inability to handle the current maintenance problem. They also realized that settling for just existing as they were would be a certain death certificate in the near future. Peacemaking is never peaceful. It always demands risk-taking.

The apostle Paul's encounter with the Corinthians was not a peaceful coexistence. Many times he placed his life and reputation on the line for the sake of the church. He combated inadequate thinking in established leadership. He held continuous dialogue with opposing leadership and refused to compromise the gospel. He was willing to pay the price of peacemaking to establish discipleship.

In the Corinthian letters, the apostle never gives specific or-

ders to go and spread the gospel. He never recites the great commission. However, ingrained within the fabric of the document
is the continuous concern for the church to be holy, and to be
reaching out to the lost. Satan has blinded many minds. Despite
the deception of darkness, the grace of God has provided the
light of the glorious gospel, and it still shines (2 Cor. 4:4-6).

Peacemaking Ethics in Conflict Resolution

Conflict resolution must incorporate an effective understanding of biblical peacemaking. The Quaker peacemaker
George Fox described the goal and virtue of peacemaking in a
letter to the king. He believed that peacemaking was the duty of
every Christian:

> The Spirit of Christ brings us to seek the peace and good of
> all men, and to live peaceably; and leads us from such evil
> works and actions as the magistrates' sword takes hold
> upon. Our desire and labour is that all who profess them-
> selves Christians may walk in the Spirit of Christ; that they,
> through the Spirit, may mortify the deeds of the flesh, and
> by the sword of the Spirit cut down sin and evil. . . . Then
> the judges and other magistrates would not have so much
> work in punishing sin in the kingdom; neither then need
> kings or princes fear any of their subjects, if they all walked
> in the Spirit of Christ; for the fruits of the Spirit are love,
> righteousness, goodness, temperance, etc. (Fox: 699).

Fox believed that faith must be aligned with daily living. A
radical faith demands a radical ideal for life. To change people's
hearts, Fox as a peacemaker paid the price by imprisonments
and persecutions. Too often pastors are unwilling to sacrifice
themselves for congregational unity. Many pastors are too concerned about acquiring high salaries, social prestige, and personal growth. That becomes a higher priority than taking the risk of
crossbearing by sacrificing for the church of God.

Today there is much laziness among pastors. It is far easier to keep busy with nonessential business than to tackle spiritual oppression, conflict, and personal spiritual accountability. The same is true with the laity. We often engage in a false notion that there is a health-and-wealth gospel proclaiming that we do not have to suffer for Christ. We become petrified in our religiosity, failing to allow the gospel to change us and our churches. We are stuck in a deadly rut.

The accomplishment of peacemaking encompasses personal accountability. Fox understood that the ethic of peacemaking demands obedience to walk in the fullness of the Holy Spirit. Peacemaking is a call to spiritual obedience in the conflicts between two spiritual kingdoms.

The causes of conflict differ from congregation to congregation, but the ingredient of all conflict involves a lessening of allegiance to God. This is often demonstrated by increasing toleration of sin. Members may elect either inwardly and personally or outwardly and vocally that they will be at peace with the world and its ideals. Then a spiritual compromise has occurred. The church has the solemn obligation to avoid these pitfalls that continually cause it to be stalemated by sin. Paul defines the gospel as a present force that calls the church to holy action against sin.

The peacemaker who is serious about the relevance of the kingdom of God in this present age must move beyond comfortable lip service to the Lord and engage in spiritual actions that challenge, restore, and are progressive in the parameters of God's love. The gospel that is now veiled to the lost must be revealed (1 Cor. 4:5). The writer of the Hebrews wrote, "Therefore, brothers and sisters, holy partners in a heavenly calling, consider that Jesus, the apostle and high priest of our confession, was faithful to the one who appointed him" (Heb. 3:1). Those desiring peace among the brothers and sisters would be wise to set their attention and desires toward Christ.

When sinful human beings focus on the purity and love of Jesus Christ, then peacemaking begins its mighty journey into our lives. There is no one who can remain in the light of God and hate the sister or brother. When we pursue the Master of all life diligently, we are either changed into his likeness or we turn away in the hardness of our hearts. Peacemakers must be conformed to the image of Christ. A congregation that doesn't seek to be transformed into the likeness of Christ will perish.

Summary: Three Parameters of Conflict

The parameter of grace: The will of God in any congregation is unchanging, whether the church is experiencing unity or disunity. God always loves his church.

1. Grace focuses the attention of the believer upon the real issues at hand and directs us to God's perfect peace.
2. Grace brings loving discipline into the church and the believer's life.
3. All ministry is dependent upon the grace of God.
4. Conflict resolution works in cooperation with the grace of God and the human demonstration of God's love.

The parameter of worship: The will of God in any congregation is for joyous worship to be the center of the Christian's life and church.

1. The focus of worship is an encounter with the cross and resurrection. This causes in each believer a celebration of thanksgiving.
2. When the celebration of worship is dulled by sin, it is hindered. God demands that his people live holy lives.
3. In joyous celebration the believer will earnestly seek a holy life, separated from unholy actions.
4. The believer must learn to imitate Christ. This becomes his ultimate worship.
5. Let us be judged by our imitation of Christ in our lives. Worship is the supreme standard of all life.
6. Wisdom in solving conflict is a gift of God.
7. Problems in the church are directly related to spiritual wisdom and spiritual ignorance.

8. Worship is feeding the spiritually ignorant that they might discover an increasing love for Christ.
9. Worship is to continue in the conflicts between spiritual kingdoms and spiritual warfare.
10. The proclamation of the gospel is an act of worship.

The parameter of peacemaking: The believer's response to God's grace and worship is demonstrated in taking action as a peacemaker.

1. The motive for peacemaking is that all believers should demonstrate that Christ is Lord of their lives.
2. Peacemaking is activity against spiritual darkness.
3. Peacemaking is dependent upon interaction between the believer and his Lord.
4. The pastor has a responsibility before God to be a peacemaker.
5. Laypeople have a responsibility before God to be peacemakers.
6. To be effective peacemakers, all God's people must live a life of godly ethics. Proper ethics are formed in a life totally dependent upon God's love and in dialogue with other believers.

CHAPTER TWO

Resolving Conflict from a Biblical Perspective

Spiritual Formation Among Peacemakers

Throughout North America thousands of congregations are seeking a new spiritual awakening. Many of these congregations have realized that such an awakening cannot be produced by programs and educational methodology. Bigger and better programs will not solve the dilemma of a society that has morally collapsed.

The solution calls for a movement of intense spiritual awakening by the Holy Spirit. It involves perceiving what we have been doing that is not working, and having vision once again to be led by the Spirit. Churchianity is dead! May it never be resurrected again! In the same way, the resolution of conflict in a local church will not occur because of goal setting, education, or anything else. It will occur when the church spiritually seeks the things of the kingdom of God. The unity of the Spirit occurs only where there is holy obedience to the Lord. There is an absence of obedience in the church today. Rather than being led by the Spirit, too many congregations are living in traditions that smother growth.

Peacemaking is both an aggressive approach to the development of holy character, and an offensive strategy against spiritual darkness. Spirituality is the only true methodology of biblical conflict resolution. This divine method of developing the ministry of the peacemaker begins with a quest to foster, implement, and prove spiritual integrity. Peacemaking is not passive. It does not sit back and feel sorry that situations exist, are causing disharmony within the church, and are disrupting our personal lives. It demands stabilization of congregational commitments to each other under the lordship of Christ. It is a spiritual yearning for Christ that invades the hearts of people. True peacemaking overcomes selfishly ambitious plans and drives for personal power and one's own fiefdom. It calls all members to be transformed into the character of Christ and to serve his kingdom.

Enthusiasm for ministry, whether lay or pastoral leadership ministry, is dependent upon spiritual honesty. Conflict resolution must confront dishonesty. Believers must struggle to submit to the truth, and then experience spiritual emancipation in the freedom of the truth. Many Christians have felt the turmoil of personal rejection by others in the spiritual war to overcome conflict. Conflict resolution is an intensive examination of values as seen in the light of the truth of the kingdom of God.

A young leader was called to pastor a suburban congregation. The previous pastor had been immoral, and the final blow came to the congregation when he was arrested for being a thief. Strong opinions were expressed at his dismissal. Some believed the devil was attacking the church and that lies were being circulated about the pastor. Others believed that the pastor was guilty. However, the facts were indisputable. The crime had been committed. A new pastor was soon assigned to the congregation.

However, the pastoral role was now held in suspicion by many people in the church. The new pastoral ministry was rejected almost immediately. The congregation was not yet ready for a new pastor. Perhaps an interim minister would have been a better idea for the church. In the midst of great congregational unrest, one vocal "saint" made it his responsibility to rid the congregation of the new pastor. There would be only one pastor, and he had been fired! Each Sunday when the new pastor would go to the pulpit to preach, the disgruntled member would deliberately stand up, make a commotion, and leave the sanctuary. The crisis continued in the congregation as people already polarized reacted violently by taking sides within the church.

The new pastor was shattered by the attacks upon him. He was being innocently crucified and chased out of the church. He did leave after a year and a half. The pastor said, "All I ever wanted to do was to love people and serve God." He let himself be destroyed by unrealistic expectations of his role in the divided congregation, and by the personal prejudices of deeply hurt people. He misunderstood the conflict and was truly broken by the attacks upon him. Many hurting pastors have not learned when to let go of situations beyond their control. They have not learned that they cannot solve every problem.

The peacemaking ministry involves establishing a healing ministry of God in the church, one that will deliver the brokenhearted to the loving care of the Lord. This care is an ointment to be administered for healing the scarred emotions of the people of God. In Luke, Jesus summarized the focus of his ministry:

> The Spirit of the Lord is upon me,
> because he has anointed me to bring good news to the poor.
> He has sent me to proclaim release to the captives
>   and recovery of sight to the blind,
>   to let the oppressed go free,
> to proclaim the year of the Lord's favor. (Luke 4:18-19)

There is a place in ministry for practical common sense. There is also a place in all of ministry for faith. In difficult situations, the understanding of what needs to be done and how to proceed can only be acquired by diligently seeking the will of God. The mission of the peacemaker is to bring peace. Yet there are people who will not become peaceable in our time of reaching out to reconcile them in difficult situations. Sometimes the peacemaker needs to wait and pray, and sometimes confrontation and action is needed. How to properly blend the two together takes help from God.

Even the Lord Jesus had opponents who would not be reconciled to him. He wisely focused his attention on those whose hearts were open to change. Many Sadducees and Pharisees went out into eternity unreconciled to God. The poor, lame, blind, and weak who believed in Jesus were born anew in the power of God. Oh, that we would have such willing hearts to be reconciled to God, and to others!

Pastors and lay leaders have a tendency to look for a mechanical methodology to remove conflict and problems from the church. Blame is often placed against this person or that person in the church. However, the biblical mandate for living the Christian life is to seek first the kingdom of God and his righteousness (Matt. 6:33). Afterward, we are to proceed in obedience to the Holy Spirit. Conflict resolution must allow people to focus their lives and hurts on the Savior's healing love. When members continue to blame each other for their problems, they will become separated from others and embittered.

There is no simple recipe for fostering peace. It is foolish to think that peace will occur when love is not present. The opposite is true, too. Love does not necessarily grow strong in a peaceful environment, in subdued places where it is not tested. True love from God grows robust when surrounded by hostility. Love is the most stubborn of all virtues. Peace occurs where love has decided to stubbornly exist despite the attacks, accusations, and sinful behavior of others. To find peace in the midst of the storm requires love that will allow self-examination, personal change, and respect for others.

Change is the most difficult part of the resolution of problems. To change, we need to break habits and transform attitudes. Peace is not produced first by others changing what they are doing. First, peace is personal. It must occur within us. Just because someone else is enjoying a peaceful life does not mean a thing to us unless we are enjoying it, too. Peace is produced when change and conformity to holiness is instituted by us. We may find ourselves totally unable to resolve conflict. The situation we are in may be beyond our control. Yet, by being at peace with God and ourselves, we can be responsible agents of redemptive love. That way, we have the inner core of peace to make peace with others, with God's strength (Matt. 5:9). "If it is possible, so far as it depends on you, live peaceably with all" (Rom. 12:18). We need to do what depends on us.

It is foolish to believe that everyone will like what we do and don't do in ministry. The servants of God must be spiritually indwelt to be God's peacemakers in a redemptive way. Peacemaking in redemption is not just putting people in a situation where they *must* get along with each other. That is not enough! To feel the effects of true fellowship with God, people must be brothers and sisters bonded together in the graciousness of the Holy Spirit. It is not possible to love God and hate our sister or brother (1 John 3:8-11).

In every mountain-size problem, the Holy Spirit will provide creative responses that allow opportunities to minister to the hurts of people. Some problems may not be worthy of devoting our emotional energy to; others demand work and faith. The fortresses of conflict will fall with a mighty thud that is sweet to God and in demonstration of his love. The Lord will never surrender his church to evil. Christ is the Lord of all the church, and we who serve him as peacemakers must have his creative thoughts. Joshua needed the instructions of "the commander of the army of the Lord" (Josh. 5:13-15). We need the instructions of the Lord for our battles, too. This is not an option for us. This is as essential to our spiritual vitality as air is to our lungs.

The church is not commissioned to shrink away because of disturbances. The Lord Jesus refused to avoid the cross by compromising his obedience to God; we are called to bear our cross in obedience, too. It is sad when a congregation becomes so lukewarm or numbed by problems that members will not hear the loving voice of the Spirit. The voice of the Spirit calls the church to spiritual honesty and truth. The Spirit calls us to love like he loves us. To recognize the voice of the Spirit speaking to us, we must walk with the One who said, "I am the way, and the truth, and the life" (John 14:6).

A church that remains unwilling to confront the real issues of their spirituality already has one foot in the grave. For example, there is a small church which has existed over a hundred years. The original founders of the church were no doubt men and women who were led by the Holy Spirit and excited about God's kingdom. Something happened about forty years ago. The church became more concerned about keeping the appearance of "peace" than about confronting sin in the lives of its membership. *Sin* became a negative word in their church conversations. Compromise became the mode of operation in the congregation. The unspoken motto of their congregational life became "Don't rock the boat."

Today, that church is nothing more than a social club with a religious title and heritage. Each week people come to the morning services, just like the previous generation. Sunday after Sunday they sing the same hymns, just as the previous generation did. If there is a single glimmer of spiritual vitality in the church, it is extremely difficult to find it. The church is spiritually dead. The spiritual honesty of the previous generation was lost when the present generation lacked commitment to spiritual truth in confronting sin.

Spiritual honesty demands a willingness to confess our sins and repent. Too many churches have become fatted cows, content on remaining outwardly peaceful at any cost. What a shame to be a fatted cow, chewing our cuds of status-quo mentality! The slaughterhouse is an ugly place to visit.

Revival is often used among evangelicals to denote what the church really needs. Do we really know what it is? Revival stirs the church until we see our deadness as a stench that is repulsive to our spiritual lives and God. The sinful odor "that clings so closely" (Heb. 12:1) comes from our worship services that are limp and lifeless, our congregational business meetings that lack spiritual breath, and our members that have no love for each other. When a church refuses to maintain love of God as a standard for all its actions, then it chooses to die. The only healthy option is for the church to be revived and have its members actively seeking for holy obedience to God in their own lives.

There is a great difference between being a peace-loving person and a peacemaker. Many people never take the action required by God to make peace an eternal reality in the lives of people. They are not peacemakers. A peacemaker stands in the harsh and cruel gap between human sinfulness and the love of God. They have understood the importance of standing firm in peacemaking so that people do not perish unreconciled to God. Love to them is more than just a nice cozy-sounding word. It is a command to lay down their lives for the well-being of others. A true peacemaker stands in the gap for people as a person who loves peace and will work for it.

Loss of Peace in the Fall

The expulsion of Adam and Eve from the garden of Eden involved a shifting of allegiance away from God (Gen. 3). Before they fell into sin, they enjoyed continuous peace with God. There was no need for peacemakers, for all was in harmony with God. The garden was a habitat of peace and love, with useful work and fellowship (3:8; 2:15, 19-20; cf. 1:26-29). There in the evening breeze, the first man and woman walked with their Creator. This fellowship, based on peace with God, was soon lost when they committed sin. Human beings became sinful, violent, disobedient, and alienated from God and each other. With their descendants, they would battle thorns and thistles as they struggled to survive apart from God; work became toil. Humanity lost the fullness that God had intended for them to enjoy forever.

Today, sin leads to entrenched conflict. Conflict becomes sin if it is not dealt with. Our sinful nature and desire to walk apart from God has left us without peace. All people have this infection caused by sin. All live in conflict with peace. John Wesley said concerning the Fall:

Accordingly, in that day [Adam] did die: He died to God—the most dreadful of all deaths. He lost the life of God: He was separated from Him, in union with whom his spiritual life consisted. The body dies when it is separated from God, . . . the soul [is distorted] when it is separated from God. But this separation from God, Adam sustained in the day, the hour, he ate of the forbidden fruit. And of this he gave immediate proof, presently showing by his behaviour, that the love of God was extinguished in his soul, which was now "alienated from the life of God." Instead of this, he was under the power of servile fear, so that he fled from the presence of the Lord. Yea, so little did he retain even of the knowledge of Him who filleth heaven and earth, that he endeavoured to "hide himself from the Lord God among the trees of the garden" (Gen. 3:8). So had he lost both the knowledge and the love of God, without which the image of God could not [properly] subsist. Of this, therefore, he was deprived at the same time, and became unholy as well as unhappy. In room of this, he has sunk into pride and self-will, the very image of the devil; and into sensual appetites and desires, the image of the beasts that perish. (*Works*, 6:67-68)

There can be no lasting resolution to conflict on earth without fellowship with God. God's standard is holiness. Sin and holiness do not mutually exist together. They are enemies with each other. Therefore, wherever sin exists, there is lack of peace among people.

Conflict resolution must recognize that this is a fallen world which is not experiencing the fullness of God's peace. At times we may sense some displays of peace in our lives, but this supply of peace is minute compared with what Adam and Eve enjoyed in the garden of Eden before the Fall. The best human intentions to foster peace fall dramatically short of the intent of God. A person who lacks peace is a poor instrument of peacemaking. The only answer to solving such inner conflicts is the intervention of God, leading to restored fellowship with God.

In every person there is a void. The void or missing ingredient to human happiness can only be filled by the presence of Jesus Christ through the Spirit. Moses pleaded with God in Exodus 33:18, "Show me your glory." The heart of Moses recognized how deficient he was compared to God's greatness. He knew firsthand the trouble sin had caused to him and Israel. The Lord graciously answered Moses in Exodus 34:5-7 by declaring his divine character of mercy and steadfast love.

The goodness of God illustrates his character. If peacemakers do not understand God's character, they will be as the blind leading the blind (Luke 6:39). God's character is compassionate, gracious, slow to anger, abounding in love for thousands, forgiving, and willing to punish sin. Peacemaking begins with a transformation into the character of God. This means that for true peace to occur, the character and image of God must be renewed and restored in human lives (Col. 3:10).

Wesley preached about a second work of grace, commonly called the baptism of the Holy Spirit, or being filled with the Spirit (Acts 1:5; 2:4; 4:31; 1 Cor. 12:13). The Holy Spirit is active in bringing every work of God's grace (Acts 2:38; Rom. 8). The fullest experience of that grace is crucial for producing a new life, and for peacemaking. Jesus came that his followers might have life "abundantly" (John 10:10). The peacemaker must be filled with the character of God and his power. To attempt peacemaking in the powerless and selfish state of the old Adamic nature is to fail. Through the cross, the second Adam, Jesus Christ, has destroyed the bondage of sin. His Spirit, who lives in the Christian, brings victory in life and peacemaking (Rom. 5).

The apostle Paul, writing to the Corinthians about their problems, declared the most excellent method for solving church division. That way is love (1 Cor. 13). The Holy Spirit fills the believer's life with divine love, which overcomes selfishness and sin.

In the sequence of Jesus' Beatitudes, we first become poor in spirit, and then we become peacemakers. Too many congregations in conflict neglect this all-important dimension of peace-making: fully yielding to the Holy Spirit through submission to the commands of Christ. The Fall has robbed humanity of peace. The cross, resurrection, and the baptism of the Holy Spirit graciously restore heavenly peace to our lives.

The Peacemaking Ministry of Jesus Christ

The ministry of Jesus Christ was and is God's provision for reconciliation through peacemaking. His ministry was the battlefield of God, to turn people from sin and being enemies of God, so that they will be reconciled to God and with each other. Jesus' ministry cannot be characterized as yielding to the status quo by compromising with sin. His was a ministry based on the absolute standards of God. Isaiah the prophet wrote of the Messiah's life as the Prince of Peace (Isa. 9:6-7). Centuries before Jesus' birth, God had promised a Christ who would be the sole monarch of the kingdom of God.

That Son of God would reign in righteousness and justice. The rebellion of Adam and Eve resulted in the loss of these qualities of life under God. Jesus Christ as the Prince of Peace came to restore what was lost, to transform people into the children of God, with their moral image once again made whole. In the synagogue at Nazareth (Luke 4), Jesus defined his mission as anointed by the Holy Spirit to preach to the world's poor, proclaim freedom to prisoners, recovery of sight to the spiritually blind, release to the oppressed, and the time of the Lord's favor.

The Lord's favor can be expressed as a transformation from bondage to peace. Jesus was instituting a call to peace. In his actions and words, he would personally be the model Peacemaker. In fact, when he was born in Bethlehem, the angels declared, "On earth peace among those whom [God] favors" (Luke 2:14). There is no peace apart from the person of Jesus Christ. He came "preaching peace" (Acts 10:36; Eph. 2:17), and "he is our peace" (Eph. 2:14). Congregations in conflict should take this to heart. Their efforts for unity will fail if they neglect the importance of seeking the leadership of the Prince of Peace. Christ alone is willing and knowledgeable in transforming the conflicts produced by people, and making peace.

Jesus' coming into the world did not mean that peace would come easily. His life was at risk soon after his birth, threatened by a king who sought to destroy him and butchered the children of Bethlehem (Matt. 2). His parents fled to another country and then returned by a safe way. Jesus' ministry was constantly harassed by Sadducees, Pharisees, scribes, soldiers, rulers, and others who sought to destroy him. Yet, in all the conflict against Jesus, he chose to love his enemies, even to the cross itself.

The Master had told his disciples that he was going away and that he would leave them a peace that was radically different from anything they had ever experienced in the world (John 14:27). On the cross, Jesus forgave his enemies and bore the sins of humanity (Luke 23:34). He became the punishment of God to people who had no peace (2 Cor. 5:21; Gal. 3:13). By his acts of love, he declared a new reign of God. Jesus would restore people to God by taking away their sins and transforming them into the children of God, with eternal peace in their souls. John 1:12 states that the transformation involves being granted the right to legally do something or be something. In this case, the act of Christ has given to us the right to become children of God and to live in his peace.

Jesus said, "Peace I leave with you; my peace I give to you. I do not give to you as the world gives. Do not let your hearts be troubled, and do not let them be afraid" (John 14:27). When Jesus spoke to his disciples, he was referring to the work of the Holy Spirit, whom he would send to them. The Spirit would teach them all things and remind them of what he had said to them (14:25-26). The Spirit would work peace in their lives.

Jesus told his disciples not to be troubled or afraid because they have a new type of peace. It will be radically different from anything ever experienced. Peace will come to us when we are obedient to Jesus' word and Spirit. This peace that Jesus offered would not only propel them through the stresses of life but would give them joy (John 14:11; 17:13). The entire New Testament church would bathe in this hope and discover it to be so powerful that it would turn the world upside down (Acts 17:6). This divine peace is needed in today's morally collapsed church. The church should be an embarrassment to this world by challenging the sins of members and of all people.

Fulfilling Jesus' Prayer for Peace in His Church

The congregation needs to develop an attitude for spiritual peace and unity. Doing this depends on each individual's willingness to submit to the lordship of Christ and his command to love one another. Jesus said, "This is my commandment, that you love one another as I have loved you" (John 15:12). This mandate was given to his followers so they could obtain the same type of love Jesus had been demonstrating to them. Such love was to be shared with others; it was not to be hoarded. The standard of this love was giving it to others. Only then would we experience the greatness of love in our own lives. This love is to be just as intense as the love Jesus and his Father had for each other (John 14:9-10).

Many theories of conflict resolution are based on a give-and-take mentality of negotiating. This is not so with regard to the kingdom of God and his church. The church is called to conform to the image of Christ (Rom. 8:29), who is the truest image of the invisible God (Col. 1:15). The church is not to conform to humanity's best notions of what peace may be. The unity of the church is decided on the basis of Christ's command for us to love one another and seek God's kingdom.

Conflict resolution is not just a matter of soothing ruffled feelings, nor of discovering creative solutions for conquering church problems, nor of finding the lowest common denominator so everyone can tolerate the selfish striving of each other. It is not mutual back-scratching. Jesus prayed for us to be unified as spiritual brothers and sisters. This means we do not have the license to use any persons or problems to excuse our unloving behavior and expressions.

Every action of Christian people must be conducted in solid spiritual honesty and oneness with Christ. Every action must be done in love. Spiritual honesty demands that there be conflict resolution methodology that faces the issues at hand, no matter how painful they may be. Jesus prayed that we might be one with him (John 17:11, 22-23). This means that we must let his actions at the cross be the governing factor in all our actions. Through his spiritual and honest love at the cross, he tells us that our actions should not incorporate half-truths and half-lies. Jesus said that only the truth would set us free (John 8:32). He personally demonstrated this premise by becoming broken on the cross to redeem fallen humanity.

There can be no compromise with evil. There must be a spiritual drive within the character of the peacemaker to rise above one's own consciousness and our deficient attitudes. The peacemaker must seek the sovereignty of God as the only source of strength for the church. The servant of God who is emptied of selfish ambition is then made spiritually fit to be a peacemaker. Should people in the midst of the heartbreak of church division be led by spiritually blinded leaders who are not in touch with God? The answer is absolutely not! Biblical conflict resolution occurs on a higher plain than what people can produce on their own. Above all things, above all personal charisma and all intellect, the peacemaker must be a searcher for God.

A law of thermodynamics states that an object in motion tends to stay in motion unless it is acted upon by an outside force. This is true in the physical world, and it is spiritually true, too. Force will produce counterforce. Conflict will produce more conflict until one opponent prevails over another. Negative attitudes and spiritual dishonesty will never produce life-changing positive hope and dreams.

The very characteristic of grace at work (discussed in the previous chapter) reminds us that God is aggressively intruding on what has been the domain of Satan. Through the cross, Jesus initiated the offensive now being conducted. The offensive is under his leadership and command. The offensive is actively tearing down walls that separate people from God and from each other (Eph. 2:11-22). The cross has produced a family bonding in the lives of millions of believers. Jesus prayed that his followers might "be one. As you, Father, are in me and I am in you, may they also be in us, so that the world may believe that you have sent me" (John 17:21).

This unity with Christ is not some hopeful never-never land. This is God's present reality, to be experienced by all who are called to his Son's love and salvation. Jesus' concern was for the church to be fully loyal to him. He concludes his prayer with a statement concerning the relationship between unity and love: "I made your name known to them, and I will make it known, so that the love with which you have loved me may be in them, and I in them" (John 17:26). Christian love is the hand that directs and provides peace and unity for repentant people.

Resolving Conflict by Redemptive Negotiation

It was an evening that the pastor and laity wished never would have happened. The church had been struggling for years to survive. After several years of feeling that he was beating his fist against a wall, the pastor with the approval of local leadership invited a denominational superintendent to address the church concerning their future. He was to propose that the remaining "faithful few" allow a neighboring congregation to transplant part of their membership into the town church as a method of reviving it.

When the meeting began, a shocked and sickening feeling developed in the small group. The pastor was immediately under attack for how he performed ministry. The issues were irrelevant to the purpose for which the meeting had been called. Scared people sidetracked the meeting to keep change from occurring. Change is often seen as a negative factor and expressed with anger. Two members verbally attacked the pastor. The pastor and his family left the meeting totally confused and hurt.

Weeks passed, and the matter continued to weigh heavily upon the congregation. Nearly six weeks later, a letter arrived for the pastor. One of his opponents wrote concerning putting the issue aside. As the pastor read the letter, he recognized an attempt to whitewash the issue at hand. The pastor wanted the issue settled, not buried unresolved. He realized that he was not defenseless in what was occurring. The pastor wanted to determine a better outcome from the conflict. He could say that everything was all right when he knew it wasn't. Or he could take a stand to teach biblical conflict resolution.

The pastor knew full well that if he insisted that members faithfully follow Matthew 18:15-20, the conflict itself could become worse. He also knew that through the years many others in the church had been victimized by people who pointed fingers at others and refused to let themselves be held accountable for their actions.

The pastor did not respond immediately to the letter. He deliberately waited for more than a week. Timing is often important in conflict resolution. It often takes time to determine a course of action and to get the right answers. While writing the letter, he was also aware there was a good chance that others would read it. He prayed over what he wrote:

> Dear _____:
>
> I have decided to respond to your letter of two weeks ago. I confess to you that I did not read it. I was too upset to do so. My wife has read it and generally told me of its contents. I will not read it because of my firm belief that such things should have been done face-to-face. You have asked for forgiveness. Consider it done. However, there are some things that should be said. I do not write these kinds of letters often. Since you decided to respond by letter, I have decided to do such too, although this is the worst way of doing it.

The first thing I wish to express is that we are brothers in Christ. Therefore, we must love one another. I have struggled here due to my anger toward you. You deeply hurt me and my family by publicly humiliating us in violation of Matthew, chapter eighteen. As you know Jesus teaches that if you have something against someone else, you are to go to them privately. You did not do that, and consequently a worse problem occurred. You deeply upset my family, to the point where I wonder if my daughter will set foot in the church again. I truly believe that you need to approach her and help her as a young woman not to lose heart. I had thought we were friends. I did not know that you were holding things against us. You also hurt my wife. I think you need to approach her, too.

I know that you are afraid of change. You have been a solid pillar of the church for years. But if there is no change, things stagnate. I have felt you working against me more than once, but always I have felt we could work through it. . . . (I know that some of the things I believe are important go against your grain.) . . .

There is another thing I think is in order. You publicly hurt us; therefore, I feel a public confession is in order. It is very difficult to stand before the congregation with this hanging over us. I am human, and I struggle to control my feelings publicly. When I am violently confronted in public, my response is and probably always will be "no response." I do this deliberately. This allows me to go over the information without committing myself until I know the facts. I did not disagree with everything you said. I disagree with how you said it. You are an excellent leader in the church. Please endeavor to speak privately to me about your concerns so that we can work it out. Matthew eighteen was designed to help people save face.

One last thing has been on my mind. Our superintendent was there to help us. We were asking him for help to keep the church alive. The actions of that night forced us not to deal with the most important issue at hand. We dealt with something altogether different. The issue was the possible transplanting of families from other churches. Did you deliberately sidetrack us? I ask this in love. Are you afraid of change and a possible loss of authority in the church? I personally do not believe you would do such a thing. But it has gone through my mind. You don't need to respond to this; just think it over. I also think that you should apologize to him, too. Sometimes in how we react to things, there is a cost to pay. I believe to really settle this means confession. As far as I am personally concerned, you are forgiven. I can't speak for others.

I have been fortunate in the last few weeks to be surrounded by brothers in Christ who have helped me to gain perspective. I am very busy. More than you will ever know. I make no apology for who I am. I am not perfect. Yet before God I stand. You, too, are not perfect. Yet before God you stand. We are brothers. Let us act as brothers in love for one another.

Pastor _____

To have spirituality in our attempts at peacemaking, we need to obey Christ's commands and instructions on settling differences among the brothers and sisters. The pastor who wrote this letter has addressed several key points that are formulated in Matthew 18:15-20. This passage shows how God's grace works in resolving conflict.

First, the process of reconciliation is to begin privately between individuals. It should never start in the public arena. In private disagreement, there is a greater latitude for discussion. When people lose face, new barriers will arise that make conflict resolution much more difficult. Trusting others and understanding what motivates others—these may never be obtained when respect for others is not granted in privacy. Private discussions can keep the issues at hand from being blown out of proportion to need. If we begin by engaging a third party in a disagreement and disregard a person's right to privacy, we will only inflict wounds. Solitary reproof is more gracious than a public rebuke.

Second in the process of reconciliation, if a member of the

church has sinned (against you), then you are to speak to that
person privately and regain the brother or sister, thus restoring
the fellowship in the church family (Matt. 18:15; earliest manu-
scripts lack "against you"; cf. 18:21). In Jesus' instructions, the
other person is the brother or sister in the church. The context of
the passage informs us that Jesus has already given a parable
about searching for a lost sheep that has gone astray (18:10-14).
Those who have gone astray must be sought or they will face the
consequences of their sin. It is wrong to pretend that we have no
need of a brother or sister with whom we disagree. The Spirit of
God has joined us together in one body (1 Cor. 12:13-30).

We must be serious about this reality of the church body and
not overlook it. When conflict destroys relationships, it is a terri-
ble situation for the entire church body. Conflict is never a private thing between people. However, there are issues that are
best negotiated privately for the sake of the entire church. Sin is
never a secret occurrence for anyone. God knows, and it always
affects others. "Be sure your sin will find you out" (Num. 32:23;
Heb. 4:12-13). Conflict that divides people is sin. It will always
ruin the fellowship enjoyed in Christ if members do not repent
and confess in the appropriate settings.

Sin grieves the Holy Spirit (Eph. 4:25-32; Heb. 12:14-17;
James 3:16—4:12). The pastor who wrote the letter attempted to
produce reconciliation by showing concern that they would remain brothers. This was a spiritual concern, and the letter was a
spiritual act on his part. True reconciliation is never just lip service to appease someone else. It is a spiritual dynamic expressed
from the heart to act as necessary for love to triumph. True reconciliation is a chance to increase love for one another. It is dependent upon forgiveness being granted between persons.

The one offended must be able to declare to the other that
they are forgiven of their transgressions because Christ has forgiven them through his atonement. The emotions must find release from hurt, and they must be healed by a Spirit-filled love
for others. This does not mean that forgiveness and forgetting

are the same thing. They are not. Forgiveness allows the hurts of the past to be healed in the light of God's grace. Human beings don't forget painful things just by deciding not to remember them any longer. Forgiveness means putting away all excuses that keep Christian sisters and brothers from producing love.

We realize that our own personal timetable for reconciliation may be unsuited to situations in the church, and our best efforts may not work. People normally must deal with issues before they can change inappropriate behavior. This may take time. It is not always accomplished immediately. An ingredient of God's love is patience, and we must use patience in relating with others (1 Cor. 13).

Third in the process of reconciliation, Jesus taught that forgiveness did not always mean letting the other person off the hook for what they had done. The issue had to be addressed, or there would be no honesty in the relationship. The pastor declared the man forgiven, as far as he was concerned. He wisely insisted on justice through wider confession, since the offense was so public. James says, "Confess your sins to one another, and pray for one another, so that you may be healed. The prayer of the righteous is powerful and effective. . . . My brothers and sisters, if anyone among you wanders from the truth and is brought back by another, you should know that whoever brings back a sinner from wandering will save the sinner's soul from death and will cover a multitude of sins" (5:16, 19-20).

The formula in Matthew 18 does not guarantee restored relationships, but it is the best way to work toward honest relationships. It is God's methodology. It is important to realize that not everything desired in conflict resolution will occur the way we want it to happen. God works with fallible people one step at a time. The above-mentioned pastor saw the letter-writing church member making an attempt to resolve the issue. One Sunday when the pastor was away, the man made a public confession of what he had done in causing conflict. He should have done this when the pastor was in the service to hear the confession.

Hence, the pastor was unable to respond in love and restore the relationship in the presence of the entire gathered church. This would have helped in the healing of the whole congregation.

Later, the layman called the pastor's daughter by phone and urged her to return to the church. The daughter took it as a half-hearted attempt. She never returned to that church. It would have been better if that layman had made a personal face-to-face visit with that daughter. In negotiations as important as this, it is always best to face each other in the love of Christ. A phone or a letter has no face. Gestures are an important part of communication. Our reaction to confession is enhanced significantly when we can read the facial expressions of the other person.

One Sunday evening after the church service, the pastor and his wife talked to the man, who offered an apology. It is important to note that some of the failure to resolve this conflict came from the pastor. He failed to define the parameters for resolution. People will always take the easiest route to try to get conflict over with; they will avoid any confrontation that may strain their emotions and strength. The layman failed, too, by not facing all those whom he had offended. In the way he handled the situation, he had a partial solution. But a partial solution is a failure when people remain separated.

In the resolving of conflict, an apology is not a biblical solution to problems. To say to someone, "I am sorry," is not what Jesus intended. Such a statement demands no response from anyone else. The proper format for confession is for the offended person to hear the person who has caused the offense say, "Will you forgive me?" This statement demands a response from the person offended. They must declare the other person forgiven or not. There are no other choices. This is the only true, biblical format for reconciliation and confession. The offended party must be allowed to respond to the offender in love.

There is an old saying that it takes two to tango. In conflict, this is not true. One person can believe in his heart that he has been injured, while the other person may be feeling good about the relationship or at least may think it is adequate. Private confrontation, "speaking the truth in love" (Eph. 4:15, 25), and confession properly done—that is what it takes to heal wounds.

Jesus insisted that when the private discussion has failed, then and only then are other spiritually minded people to become involved. Again, the assumption for this phase of resolution is privacy, this time with a select small group of counselors. Several years ago a pastor spoke at special meetings in the church he was serving. Afterward, one person was offended by what took place and felt that the pastor didn't like him, but said nothing to the pastor about it. One day the pastor received a phone call from a church leader asking if they could meet together to discuss the problem. The pastor had no idea there was a problem. A meeting was scheduled.

It didn't take long for news of the meeting to spread throughout the congregation. The pastor began to receive phone calls from people who were telling him that they would be at the meeting. What he had thought was going to be a private meeting had become newsworthy. The meeting went well, and when it was over, all had hearts that were united in love. This does not always happen. Perhaps a greater understanding of each other could have occurred in privacy. The large-group meeting did not allow such intimacy.

Jesus was concerned that others should refrain from "meddling" unless asked to be involved by those who had failed to resolve the issue or by others who could no longer ignore the problems. I am sure the group of laypeople who came together had godly concern for each other and were willing to show their love by physical support. We give them an A+ for this action. However, it might have seemed like a power bloc. There was a loss of the intimacy that could have bonded them all closer together in love. When it is necessary for others to be involved, they should be spiritually minded mediators (Gal. 6:1-2). Spiritually bonded mediators are not to stand in judgment or to choose sides. Their role should be to help both sides in the controversy to understand what is occurring in their relationship with each other and before God (Matt. 18:16).

A young man who was preparing for pastoral ministry was working his way through school in a local store where several Christian employees worked. The owner of the store began to notice expensive items missing. One day one of the Christian employees heard the young man admitting to stealing the items. The Christian was shocked and greatly upset that the young man was a thief. At first the Christian did not know how to respond. He was caught off guard. He was disturbed that the young man had stated that he would not return the items.

The Christian began to pray, and the Spirit of God would not give him rest over the situation. The Christian employees were informed and secretly began praying for the young man. Several of them went to the man and demanded that he make restitution. At first he refused. They then told him that if he didn't return the items stolen, they would tell the entire church. Thirty days were given him to pay for the items he had stolen.

During the time of tension, the non-Christian employer found out what the Christians were doing. He allowed them to proceed without prosecuting the thief. The employer witnessed that God's people have a standard to live by and will do what is right. The bill was paid, though one wonders whether the young man repented of his sin or paid the bill only because of pressure placed on him by the Christian employees. Many times in conflict resolution, questions involving hidden thoughts and motivations are difficult to discover and understand.

The believers who confronted the young man did so privately, though there was a threat of public disclosure of sin. Again, privacy is an important tool in conflict resolution. Negotiators should have a reputation of being tight-lipped. No gossips should be allowed to participate. The aim of conflict resolution and negotiation is restoration to the body of Christ and to the Lord. The law of Moses states that whenever there is an accusation against someone, it must be affirmed by two or three witnesses. Moses was given that format to assure order and the preservation of truth. The witnesses were to prove the truth. The witnesses that Jesus insisted upon were to make sure that what took place between the two persons was truthful.

The final step that Jesus insisted upon to resolve conflict was to disclose the truth to the entire church. This is a touchy issue, due to the increased number of legal suits brought against churches. Telling the church about failure in resolution is not a punishment. It is an enlistment of the entire body to pursue restoration. Every member of the congregation is responsible before God to seek the well-being of others. The church must bear one another's burdens and thus fulfill the law of Christ (Gal. 6:2). If this step in restoration fails, then the response of the church must be the excommunication of the offender from the fellowship of the body of Christ. This becomes the punishment when all attempts toward reconciliation are rejected.

It is not uncommon for people to become angry over situations, break with a congregation, and take their problems to other congregations. It is easy for someone to switch church attendance to another congregation. If a church has a habit of responding to such things with an attitude that what is out of sight is left out of mind, then nothing will be resolved, and sin will continue raping the congregation. The church must act responsibly for the sake of the larger church of Jesus Christ.

The apostle Paul writes about a man who has had sexual relations with his father's wife (1 Cor. 5:1-5). The church had failed to resolve the issue, and the man refused to repent. Paul's instructions are as follows:

First, when the church is assembled, they are to act in the name of the Lord Jesus. The church at Corinth was probably not a large one. The Corinthian believers belonged to several house churches. When they gathered together in the various places of worship, they needed to recognize that what was done in the name of Jesus affected all of them.

Second, the discipline of the man and woman in sin is a responsibility of the whole church. We assume that at this point in time, the instructions of Matthew 18 have failed and excommunication is the only option left for the Corinthian house churches. This action of the church is done only in the authority of Christ. In the power of the spiritual union provided by Christ through the Holy Spirit, Paul will join with the believers in their action as a unified body. He will be with them in his spirit.

Third, the church is to formally turn the man over to Satan for the destruction of the flesh, so that his spirit may be saved. It is the hope and prayer of the church that through this action, the man will see the consequences of his sin and repent. The church always has a mission for restoration.

In another unhappy encounter with a sinful church member, Paul instructs the church that their punishment has been enough. Apparently the sinner has repented, and they are to restore the sinner to fellowship in the church. They are to reaffirm their love (2 Cor. 2:5-11). In all church discipline, there must be hope that the lost will repent. The pastor mentioned earlier (who wrote the letter for reconciliation) never reached the level of enlisting help for true reconciliation. The woman in the first chapter was never confronted by the church and never confessed her sin; hence, she never experienced the love of the church at its best.

True love must often pursue tough and hard roads to produce fruit. Many earthly parents have had to stand firm against poor conduct by their offspring, for their children's well-being. Many parents have never been appreciated for what they did for their children until much later. This is true in church conflict resolution, too. Church people too often do not follow through in obeying Jesus' instructions in Matthew 18:15-20. They hope for the best, but they achieve the worst when they don't follow that guide. Jesus' instructions are not simply suggestions for conduct. They are legal mandates for the church under the leadership of the kingdom of God proclaimed and inaugurated by Jesus. In baptism, we have pledged to do what Jesus commands, and we need to fulfill our vows (Matt. 28:20). We need to act in obedience and true love.

At the beginning of this chapter, we noted that thousands of congregations are praying for a spiritual awakening. Spiritual honesty, mandated by God, will be a part of a revived church. To be revived, the church must confront its sinful actions. Judgment does begin with the household of God (1 Pet. 4:17).

In Matthew 5, Jesus adds to this method of conflict resolution: "When you are offering your gift at the altar, if you remember that your brother or sister has something against you, leave your gift there before the altar and go; first be reconciled to your brother or sister, and then come and offer your gift" (5:23-24). We are to take the initiative in restoring the relationship if the fellow member thinks we have done something wrong, even if we think we are in the right. Only when that is done can we worship properly.

Thus, in Matthew 18:15-20 we are told that if someone has trespassed (against us), we are to go and be reconciled. In Matthew 5:23-24 we are told that if someone has something against us, we are to go and be reconciled. In Matthew 18:10-15 we are told to seek the lost one that has gone astray (cf. Gal. 6:1-2; James 5:19-20). So whether we have offended another, or have been offended by another, or otherwise notice a fellow member sinning—in each case, we are commissioned to take the initiative and go to the brother or sister to make peace and restore the lost. "Pursue peace with everyone, and the holiness without which no one will see the Lord" (Heb. 12:14). This is the Rule of Christ for us to follow.

Each member of the body of Christ has a responsibility to correct brothers and sisters who have sinned. Paul says, "My friends, if anyone is detected in a transgression, you who have received the Spirit should restore such a one in a spirit of gentleness. Take care that you yourselves are not tempted" (Gal. 6:1). All Christians have received the Spirit, so all share this task. Yet within the church are special resources for reconciliation which need to be identified, gifted "spiritual" helpers (Gal. 6:1, KJV).

When there is great imbalance of power, as in cases of abuse, it may not be safe or wise for the victim to go to the offender; a skilled counselor-protector is needed to take charge of the healing process. Jesus and Paul spoke out forcefully in behalf of the victimized (Matt. 15:4-6; 18:6-7; 18:13-15; 23:4, 15; Luke 7:36-50; Acts 16:16-18). The Scripture will not let us be concerned only about offenses against ourselves, when our own toes are tramped on. We need to care for victims *and* for offenders, to work for healing and restoration.

How can people be restored to fellowship with the church and with the Lord? This is only accomplished by honest communication, done in the love and integrity of the Lord, and with the strength and gentleness of God's Spirit.

Peace Through Spiritual Brokenness

There are times in the Christian life when good people reach a point of feeling like they have more problems than they can handle. Their frustrations with the sorrows of life can flow over into their church life. Anger is often transferred to the congregational setting and expressed there.

Several years ago a small suburban church was explosively divided over change and doctrinal issues. The crisis forced the denominational leaders to remove the pastor. Church attendance dropped dramatically from 120 to 35 bewildered souls on Sunday mornings. A new pastor was called to replace the previous one. When the church board met, it was decided to send letters to everyone who had left the church, urging them to return. The letter also stated that if anyone needed to talk to the new pastor about the situation, they should contact him for an appointment.

After the letters were mailed, Bill and Susy called the new pastor. They were upset over what had occurred. When the pastor arrived at their home, he was immediately bombarded with accusations against "those people" who had done this and that in the crisis. The couple vented much anger, and no immediate remedy was to be found. Perhaps Bill and Susy didn't want a remedy. They were unforgiving, and they were hurt. They were in sin, but they were not there alone. The thirty-five who stayed in the church plus the sixty-five who had left were in sin, too. They had all failed to preserve the bond of peace and the unity of the Holy Spirit. The flock had scattered, and many were deeply wounded. Some would never be involved in any church again.

Yet in the midst of this tragedy, it is also true that God's grace is operating and persistently searching the hearts of people to redeem them from their sins. It is dangerous to sever fellowship with a church because sin is directing lives. The sin should be confronted. Angry division is not natural in the kingdom of God. Many depart from the faith because, discouraged about conflict, they fail to belong and participate regularly in any local church.

How can such a crisis be overcome? How can ordinary people experience healing so intensive that they reclaim and reaffirm their love for the local church? The answer lies in brokenness before the Lord, both individually and corporately as the body of Christ. Pain and hurt should not be confused with brokenness. Brokenness is more than just hurting or being filled with tears. It is acknowledgment that apart from the grace and mercy of God, we are extremely weak and sinful.

Brokenness is a tool God uses in our lives first to correct ourselves before we can help others. Brokenness is personal and frightening. We who are broken before God volunteer to participate in possible suffering. We engage in intensive introspection of who we are in relationship to Jesus Christ and others. We realize that our love is faulty and that we need to consecrate our love as Jesus loves others. We learn to empty personal selfishness so that we may be filled with godly selflessness. We inwardly declare total dependence on God and love for God when all human efforts seem impossible. We have faith that Jesus Christ can never be defeated in what he is doing for us and his church.

Brokenness is extremely painful and yet absolutely necessary for our well-being. It is an abandonment of our pride so that the Lord Jesus can fully live in us. Our pride is ugly to behold when illuminated by divine and pure light. When self is in charge of our lives and church, then our personal lives have no room for spiritual leadership and guidance. Selfishness will always wage war against the Spirit. The flesh and the Spirit will always battle, and the result will be disastrous unless there is full surrender to Christ's lordship in our lives. This is one of the chief reasons for church crises. When pastors and laypersons fail to walk in the Spirit, the results are the works of selfishness.

Galatians 5:19-21 lists various sins of the flesh: adultery, fornication, impurity, licentiousness, idolatry, sorcery, enmities, strife, jealousy, anger, quarrels, dissensions, factions, envy, drunkenness, carousing. Paul warns that those who practice such things will not inherit the kingdom of God. In these verses he is describing the world, and I am convinced that he is describing anyone who does not walk with the Spirit of God. Whoever is not walking in the Spirit is walking in selfishness.

A constant need is for us to restore others in a spirit of gentleness (Gal. 6:1). Brokenness is tough to live out. To achieve our desires, we need to rely not on human effort but on spiritual emancipation. Brokenness is voluntarily lowering the comfort zones surrounding our lives so we can be directed and disciplined by the Lord. In other words, we have a responsibility in brokenness to submit obediently to God in everything. God has a responsibility to change us into the image of Christ. In brokenness, we consciously seek fellowship with God, and this demands fellowship with others. The result of brokenness is a desire to lay hold of God.

This brokenness occurs when we are confronted with the cross. The cross is the place where human selfishness is destroyed. It is also the place where our human wills come into conflict with the great truth, that sin brings death and destruction. Sin is totally ugly and undesirable for a holy life. When such knowledge impacts a human heart, a heart-wrenching crisis occurs. In this crisis, human brokenness leads believers to consecrate themselves to God.

We are responsible before God to have a consecrated life, and God reacts by spiritually sanctifying believers in lives of the Holy Spirit's purity and empowerment. Jesus endorses this when he calls his followers to deny themselves, take up their cross, and follow him. This call is recorded in all three of the synoptic Gospels (Matt. 16:24-26; Mark 8:34-38; Luke 9:23-26). Our eternal destiny depends on our response.

How can church division be stopped? We must initiate a desire among God's people to submit to the lordship of Christ and to affirm the uniqueness of the body of Christ. How can we experience healing from painful hurts in the church? The process begins with brokenness, full submission to God, and trusting God to change our hearts. First our own hearts need to be changed before we invite others to change.

The Holy Spirit's role in conflict resolution is twofold. First, the Spirit works upon our hearts to deliver us from sin. Second, the Spirit changes others. If we think peacemaking is just for the other fellow, we are mistaken. The Spirit searches the deep things hidden within human hearts (Rom. 8:26-27; 1 Cor. 2; cf. Heb. 4:12-13). This encounter with the Spirit is always an encounter with agape love.

Matthew (chaps. 5 and 18) tells us to go and be reconciled with our sisters and brothers. Brokenness before God and sensitivity to the Spirit is the necessary ingredient for all church efforts toward unity. In brokenness, we become pliable for change. No one can force another person to change. We only have control of ourselves. Matthew 18 can help in restoring fellowship, but without a change in our inner being, we will not experience true reconciliation. We must change even if others do not!

Dying to ourselves in brokenness is not something that we do once in our lives. It is a "daily" bearing of our crosses for Christ's sake (Luke 9:23). It is having the same attitude that Jesus Christ had when he went to the cross, as Paul says:

Let the same mind be in you that was in Christ Jesus,
   who, though he was in the form of God,
      did not regard equality with God
      as something to be exploited,
   but *emptied himself,* taking the *form of a slave,*
      being born in human likeness.
   And being found in human form,
      he *humbled himself*
      and became *obedient to the point of death—*
      even death *on a cross.*
   Therefore God also highly exalted him
      and gave him the name that is above every name,
   so that at the name of Jesus every knee should bend,
      in heaven and on earth and under the earth,
   and every tongue should confess that Jesus Christ is Lord,
      to the glory of God the Father.
                              (Phil. 2:5-11, italics added)

Paul told the Philippian church that everyone should follow the model of Christ's obedience and love. He also encourages them to "work out [their] own salvation with fear and trembling" (Phil. 2:12). Notice the *italicized words* (above) as keys to understanding the attitude of Jesus Christ, the attitude that we must have in our lives, too. Christ's character must be found in every believer. He had heart-breaking encounters when he lived on the earth, and so will we. If we want godly solutions to our problems, we must plan to imitate his life. He also lived the only sinless and perfect life (Heb. 4:15; Rom. 3:23).

The development of Christlikeness in our lives occurs primarily through suffering. Suffering is like a refining fire, removing the slag in our lives and freeing the refurbished person to emerge creatively in Christ. The servant of God, when totally submissive to this process of refinement and open to the role of suffering, will discover a personal adventure into spiritual growth and development. Even when surrounding circumstances speak in contrary fashion, we can find joy in the soul, put there by God.

Let's take this one step further: The peacemaker needs spiritual wisdom to succeed. James 3:17-18 describes the wisdom that God graciously gives his faithful children: "But the wisdom from above is first pure, then peaceable, gentle, willing to yield, full of mercy and good fruits, without a trace of partiality or hypocrisy. And a harvest of righteousness is sown in peace for those who make peace." The peacemaker hungers for divine wisdom because it is pure.

Conflict resolution cannot be built on falsehood. It must be founded on what is pure. The wisdom of Christ is pure, and it alone provides the foundation for successful peacemaking. Purity becomes for the believer the evidence of the indwelling of the Holy Spirit. The Spirit grants to weak people a purity of heart that is aligned with the heart and wisdom of God. This purity is further characterized by peacefulness, gentleness, submissiveness, mercy, good fruits, impartiality, and truthfulness. Where there is a lack of purity, there must be a return to the purity of God for people to be truly transformed in their relationships with each other.

Peacemakers must have the support of the Savior if they are to succeed. The Savior demands purity of heart. Jesus says, "Blessed are the pure in heart, for they will see God. Blessed are the peacemakers, for they will be called children of God" (Matt. 5:8-9). The health of the Christian's spiritual life is more important than devising some checklist strategy for solving conflict. All good things must flow from the heart. True biblical peacemaking must be considered a holy undertaking by God. People cannot accomplish even the most minute resolution of conflict without personally walking in the holy way. Good trees produce good fruit. Bad trees cannot produce good fruit (Matt. 7:15-20; cf. 15:10-20). Peacemaking must be pure and good in everything. Spiritual honesty is directly related to the integrity of the heart.

The Personal Brokenness of God's Peacemakers

As explained, the ministry of peacemaking is a call to seasons of suffering. This is the personal discovery of spiritual brokenness. It is the realization that all suffering will one day cease when Jesus Christ returns for his church. In this interlude between the cross and the Lord's return, peacemakers must engage in radical intercession wherever there is human misery and crises. It is a call to complete discipleship. There is no immunity granted to the peacemaker that will repeal the hurts of life.

Jesus says, "If any want to become my followers, let them deny themselves and take up their cross daily and follow me. For those who want to save their life will lose it, and those who lose their life for my sake will save it" (Luke 9:23-24). Jesus insists that his disciples deny themselves and focus their complete attention upon the kingdom of God. He insists that they carry the cross assigned to them. The cross must be understood to be a lonely, tough, and destructive instrument of justice. In terms of the kingdom of God, Jesus says, "Every day you must be willing to die for me."

Although Jesus calls us to die with him, it is sometimes tougher to live with him. Our lives are no longer focused on selfishness, but on his promises of love. Those promises push us onward in a triumphal procession of his grace (2 Cor. 2:14-16). In the Roman world, once a person was nailed to a cross, he stayed there until he died, even if it took several days. He experienced much pain on the cross. The disciples of Jesus were required to yield everything they possessed for Christ and the kingdom of God. They were required to be emotionally and spiritually crucified, and sometimes physically. Paul says, "I have been crucified with Christ; and it is no longer I who live, but it is Christ who lives in me" (Gal. 2:19-20). The cross was a place of self-death so that the Christ life might be raised in us.

These are some of the toughest words that Jesus ever spoke. He leaves no middle ground when it comes to what he expects in commitment. The apostle Peter writes, "For to this you have been called, because Christ also suffered for you, leaving you an example, so that you should follow in his steps" (1 Pet. 2:21). The peacemaker's journey of faith is directed into the valley of suffering and brokenness.

In suffering, peacemakers will receive little recognition for what they have done. Theirs is a journey of learning godly humility as they focus their entire life upon the presence of Jesus Christ, who is living within. In fact, when praised by others, they will immediately glorify God. Human praise will at times seem distasteful for they long to hear only the words of the Lord, "Well done, good and trustworthy slave; . . . enter into the joy of your master" (Matt. 25:21). True peacemakers will no longer belong to the folly and disease of the sin of the world. They have deliberately separated themselves from that to belong to God.

Peacemakers will discover four great truths in their work. First, as obedient disciples of Jesus Christ, they will discover that the suffering of others cannot be fully understood unless they personally suffer. Peacemakers cannot stand near the sidelines of the battle and scream encouragements to those being bombarded with trials unless they suffer, too. There must be a spiritual bonding with others in sorrow. This bonding is necessary if unity of fellowship and joy are to be experienced. A church depressed by years of struggle cannot relate to a pastor who has never hurt.

Jesus is our example in conquering of suffering. Hebrews 4:14-15 states, "Since, then, we have a great high priest who has passed through the heavens, Jesus, the Son of God, let us hold fast to our confession. For we do not have a high priest who is unable to sympathize with our weaknesses, but we have one who in every respect has been tested as we are, yet without sin."

Second, suffering is not totally an individual experience. In the body of Christ, no one is allowed to secretly suffer. When one person suffers, the entire body of Christ feels the pain (1 Cor. 12:26; Rom. 12:15). In the same way, an entire congregation, when divided and in crisis, will have pain that is felt by other congregations. Others will feel the strain in the larger family of God. Peacemaking is radical ministry because it declares that we are willing to experience hurt, and even to be destroyed, if such a sacrifice will build others into Christlikeness and bring glory to God (Rom. 9:3; Exod. 32:32). This is a mystery, yet true.

Third, suffering is an experience in spiritual formation that allows the participant in suffering to discover total reliance on God. Disciples learn that the glitter of the world has no place in their lives. Like Abraham of long ago, disciples look for a city built by God (Heb. 11:10). They know that in the hurts of life, their only consolation is to dwell with Christ in his perfect will. They will learn that the pruning of the Lord to bring better fruit in their lives is a great blessing.

Fourth, our personal suffering for Christ will not be understood by others, and in many circumstances the peacemaker will receive unjust criticism. There are no walls in our lives that will be unchallenged by the enemies of the cross, or by well-intentioned people. They will scrutinize and criticize our lives. Many battles will be fought that will personally be distasteful. The truth is that there will be wounds, but we know that "all who want to live a godly life in Christ Jesus will be persecuted" (2 Tim. 3:12).

James 1:2 may well become the theme of life: "My brothers and sisters, whenever you face trials of any kind, consider it nothing but joy." Peacemaking through trials forces the Christian to rely solely on the grace of God for success and for the future. In the deserts of trials and despair, the unique gifting of the Holy Spirit will bloom for the good of the entire church. Indeed, God has chosen the foolish things of the world to confuse the inferior wisdom of the world's system in rebellion toward God (1 Cor. 1:19-21). Persecution will always arise against the godly, but in the power of the Holy Spirit, the servant of God will arise victorious and strong, in depending upon God's power.

Paul's Brokenness Before God in Ministry

In leading the church at Corinth, the apostle Paul personally knew what it meant to suffer. In 2 Corinthians 1:3-11, he identifies with the church by mentioning his personal suffering. Among Corinthian believers, there is disagreement over Paul's role in the church. Some think they are Paul's benefactors, with the responsibility to support Paul as anyone pays a hired employee. Paul agrees that he has the right to food and drink. Yet he sees the Corinthians as immature in Christ, perhaps thinking they can buy Paul and his gospel. To illustrate God's grace, Paul offers the gospel free of charge (1 Cor. 9:4-18). He believes that his only benefactor is God. God is the one who will support the work of Christ through Paul, not the Corinthians—though he does ask them to give for the poor saints at Jerusalem (1 Cor. 16:1-4; 2 Cor. 8–9).

The enemies of the gospel use Paul's refusal to be supported as an accusation that he has dishonest motives. Paul defends the gospel by declaring to the Corinthians that they should not be ashamed of his sufferings. They are to rejoice that together they can work for God's kingdom. God has chosen to use weak people to promote his love. Paul tries to win an audience with the Corinthians by reminding them of his sufferings for Christ. The apostle realizes that he must gain this hearing to help establish a pure gospel. In the church, he must battle for the church.

In 2 Corinthians 1:8, Paul states, "We do not want you to be unaware, brothers and sisters, of the affliction we experienced in Asia; for we were so utterly, unbearably crushed that we despaired of life itself." In Paul's ministry of apostleship, he had reached the point of pressure upon him being so great that he did not have the human strength to endure it. He had despaired even of life. The personal pressure upon him was so overwhelming that he believed that he would die. He was under the sentence of death, with only a temporary reprieve.

Paul's opponents were painting a picture of apostleship that honored strength rather than weaknesses (1 Cor. 4:8-13). Paul states that his sufferings have forced him to rely on God rather than on himself. He says that the God who showed great power by raising Christ from the dead is working a new life in him (2 Cor. 1:9). His apostleship is proof of divine ordination. The Corinthians are the living proof of God working through Paul. He endured his sufferings in obedience to Christ. They were symbols of the power of God to work in weak vessels (4:7-12).

Suffering should never be a guideline to determine if someone is or is not in the will of God in ministry. It is what happens to the sufferer in relationship to Christ that will determine if the power of God is being demonstrated. Our natural response is to avoid suffering. Paul does not enjoy suffering, but he will not retreat from it. To retreat would be self-defeating. It would result in a pity party. Paul's determination is not to be conquered, but in the power of God to challenge all untruthfulness, and to totally rely upon God to win the Corinthians back to true faith.

The church does not belong to the Corinthians, nor to Paul. The church benefactor is God, and it exclusively belongs to God. God is the one who directs the callings of his believers. A old hymn says: "God leads his dear children along, some through the waters, some through the flood, some through the fire, but all through the blood, some through great sorrow, but God gives a song, in the night season and all the day long." For Paul, suffering is a refinement unto the glory of God and his power.

Paul is determined to make it clear that his adequacy to declare the gospel comes solely from God. His power to preach is given from God. This is a gift, and he refuses to credit himself for his accomplishments. Paul has faced accusations that his humility is a front for a deceptive agenda. He views his sufferings as a contrast between human despair and spiritual victory:

> We are afflicted in every way, but not crushed;
>   perplexed, but not driven to despair;
>   persecuted, but not forsaken;
>   struck down, but not destroyed;

> always carrying in the body the death of Jesus,
> so that the life of Jesus
>   may also be made visible in our bodies. (2 Cor. 4:8-10)

Paul tells the Corinthians that he will not give up because of suffering. He has had a radical transformation by Christ that gives him victory. The Corinthians can enjoy the same transformation into spiritual victory. Paul concludes these thoughts by a statement of faith: "So we do not lose heart. Even though our outer nature is wasting away, our inner nature is being renewed day by day" (2 Cor. 4:16). His sufferings are intense, but his faith is the factor that transports him onward into ministry. In speaking of the Corinthians, he shares the encouragement he has received: "I am filled with consolation; I am overjoyed in all our affliction" (7:4). Paul had been greatly discouraged and extremely sad prior to the Lord's deliverance in the situation. Paul experienced all the emotions common to life, yet in his faith he kept his life targeted on the holiness of God. He refused to surrender his calling.

Summary

We have discussed two great principles that must be incorporated into the practice and lifestyle of the church. First, our outward methodology for resolving issues begins with obedience to the biblical truths found in Matthew 18:15-20.

Second, the Holy Spirit works with us through our obedience and leads us to spiritual brokenness. This is done so that the Spirit might restore holiness within us. To succeed, all conflict resolution must be built on the brokenness of the peacemakers.

Brokenness forces the parties involved in conflict to become open to each other as servants of God. When our attitudes depict godly servanthood, then our self has no room to dictate the results of conflict resolution. We become attuned to God's will and not selfish in what we do. The result is that the resolution will not glorify us or the other person. It will glorify God and build up the church.

In this chapter we also sketched out some of the parameters of peacemaking. Peacemaking is:

1. An aggressive approach to develop holy character, and an offensive strategy against spiritual darkness.
2. Not passive, but a persistent undertaking of the work of God in our behalf.
3. Concerned with displaying love modeled after Christ, love which must grow even in nonpeaceful church settings.
4. Examining ourselves with God's love. It is a demand for personal change, and for us to respect others.
5. Experiencing firsthand the importance of being a peacemaker indwelt with the Holy Spirit.
6. Discovering that the ministry of Jesus Christ is transformational. People can be changed into Christlikeness.
7. Living a life of spiritual honesty.
8. Using the methods of Jesus as described in Scripture and particularly in Matthew 18, to settle disagreements in the church.
9. Self-examination leading to brokenness. Spiritual brokenness and suffering will lead us to spiritual enhancement. Some people may not understand this work of God in our lives, but the God who raises the dead is with us.

CHAPTER THREE

Peacemaking and War Against the Church

Warnings of Attacks Against the Church

There are two major levels of conflict in the church. The first level involves disagreements between believers when they all have a spiritual desire to please God and work out resolution. This is called internal conflict resolution This type of conflict resolution is achieved through spiritual brokenness and by following the teachings of Jesus recorded in Matthew 18:15-20. The second level of conflict involves deliberate attacks against believers and their faith. In this type of conflict, others attack believers' credibility as possessors of the love of God in the world. This is called external conflict resolution. Many crises recorded in the New Testament involved both types of conflict.

Believers at Corinth did not understand the motives of other believers as in the case of eating meat offered to idols (1 Cor. 8, 10). Paul was forced by the spiritual and emotional sensitivity levels of the believers to provide a viable resolution of the concerns over which the believers were in conflict. This was an internal matter in the church, and hence we shall call it internal conflict resolution.

In addition, the church found itself assaulted by false apostles deliberately trying to destroy the reputation of the apostle Paul and gain selfish control of the church. This conflict was created by those who were not truly part of God's church, and it touched the lives of the Lord's faithful servants who were trying to make sense of the problems they faced. Hence, the apostle

Paul was forced to deal with external and internal conflict.

New Testament church life was never one of solitary existence and thus was often not peaceful. The earliest church found itself in the midst of battles to prove to the world the integrity of Christianity. Biblical Christianity does not retreat to places of solitude, seeking to avoid human misery. It engages in an active denunciation of society's evils by proclaiming the love of God for sinful people. It issues the summons of Almighty God for repentance and faith.

Jesus' Warnings About Attacks from Outside

Jesus repeatedly warned his disciples that the church had enemies who would try to control and destroy it. The previous chapter dealt with biblical guidelines for resolving conflict from inside the church. This chapter will deal with the worst-case scenario of direct assaults upon the church by those outside the church.

In Matthew 7:15-23, Jesus speaks of attacks against the church:

> Beware of false prophets, who come to you in sheep's clothing but inwardly are ravenous wolves. You will know them by their fruits. Are grapes gathered from thorns, of figs from thistles? In the same way, every good tree bears good fruit, but the bad tree bears bad fruit. A good tree cannot bear bad fruit, nor can a bad tree bear good fruit. Every tree that does not bear good fruit is cut down and thrown into the fire. Thus you will know them by their fruits.
>
> Not everyone who says to me, "Lord, Lord," will enter the kingdom of heaven, but only the one who does the will of my Father in heaven. On that day many will say to me, "Lord, Lord, did we not prophesy in your name, and cast out demons in your name, and do many deeds of power in your name?" Then I will declare to them, "I never knew you; go away from me, you evildoers."

Jesus places his disciples on alert against false prophets and their doctrines. With their deceptions in the church, they would try to devalue Jesus' reputation as the Bringer of truth, salvation, and obedience to God. By his warning, Jesus instructs his disciples to guard themselves from the intrusion of false prophets, and to be alert in recognizing these enemies of the faith. They will be identified by the type of fruit they are producing.

The fruit that Jesus is speaking about is the fruit of the Holy Spirit, expressions of "love, joy, peace, patience, kindness, generosity, faithfulness, gentleness, and self-control" in the lives of believers (Gal. 5:22). Such fruit is the best evidence of the Holy Spirit's work among Christians. The Holy Spirit's mode of operation is always of the highest ethical and moral fiber. This ethic is rooted in Christlikeness and spiritual honesty. Jesus said, "I am the way, and the truth, and the life. No one comes to the Father except through me" (John 14:6).

The very fact that Jesus came preaching a gospel of repentance and reconciliation is a revelation that God has declared his heart of love to humanity. God has done so with the highest degree of truth and ethics. God's purpose is for Christ to invade every segment of the world by demonstrating his character in the church, through the fruit of God's Spirit. Christ has set the church free from sin and bondage, to call people from evil-prone behavior to holy participation with God. The church is to do the deeds of Christ in the world. Each believer has received the redemptive work of Christ and now has a moral relationship with the neighbor. The gospel sets people free to be honest.

The proof of our spiritual honesty is the manifestation of these fruits of holiness. To be consistent, love must be honest. Love must be demonstrated by following the model of Christ in all our responses toward the woes of human life. This means that the Christian cannot sit back when the neighbor is suffering. There is no room for inactivity against suffering in the Christian lifestyle. This imitation of Christ is an all-consuming quest to live each day in the sovereign will of the Holy Spirit.

When obedience to this lifestyle is maintained and not violated by sin, then the fruits of Christlikeness will increase in the believer's life. Jesus spoke of a good tree bearing only good fruit. It is impossible for false prophets and enemies of the cross to bear good fruit because their lives are characterized by evil. They produce works of evil: "adultery, fornication, impurity, licentiousness, idolatry, sorcery, enmities, strife, jealousy, anger, quarrels, dissensions, factions, envy, drunkenness, carousing, and things like these" (Gal. 5:19-21, KJV/NRSV).

When falseness first touches the church, it at first may not appear harmful. It is deceptive. It may look good because it excites people. However, with their religiosity, these slick deceivers are like wolves ready to destroy the flock of God. They will attempt to destroy whoever opposes their plans. They are violent, sinful instruments of Satan, and spiritually blind, hating the light of God. The church may initially appear helpless and weak in comparison to the power of the wolves, but the Great Shepherd protects them (John 10:11-18; 17:9-15). Through the Spirit and the victory of Christ, God will not only warn believers of danger. By his powerful grace he will also provide a way to triumph over the attacks of the enemies of the church (1 Cor. 10:13).

The church needs to be on alert, watching for the intrusion of false prophets. That is far better than for members to find themselves in a crisis of trying to restore unity after the destructive forces of the church's enemies have caused chaos. Churches that stay alert are less likely to be destroyed by false doctrines and disagreements.

There can be no compromise with falsehood. The kingdom of God is always violently opposed to the kingdom of darkness. Believers are to guard their own lives from the works of the flesh. Evil works are forbidden to those who walk by the leading of the Holy Spirit. In their very foundation, fleshly ways are extremely corrosive and destructive. Christians have been made to walk by the great leading of the Holy Spirit, under the lordship of Christ. The works of the flesh lead only to spiritual death.

Jesus ordered the disciples to center their lives in a quest to bear good fruit, and to carry out his work throughout the world (Matt. 28:18-20). Our peacemaking decisions must bear witness to the need of reconciliation for church unity. It must also testify that all human wholeness must be joined to the commandment of Jesus recorded in John 15:12: "This is my commandment, that you love one another as I have loved you. No one has greater love than this, to lay down one's life for one's friends."

Wise persons will heed Jesus' instruction to guard their ways against evil. They will seek and acquire the fruits of God's holy character when the winds of adversity pound against them. They must seek the kingdom of God and his love above everything else in life. They have built their lives on a sure foundation of truth and honesty, which is Christ himself. Yet in all of this, we know that our peacemaking decisions cannot always be perfect. We are influenced by a fallen world and culture. But we bear witness to the ultimate reality of God's love and ministry of reconciliation.

Our peacemaking decisions go beyond human endeavors by declaring the vision of God to reconcile people. This vision of the grace of God at work allows those in conflict to repent and receive forgiveness in the integrity of God, who is Truth above all else. Consequently, the role of the church in conflict resolution is more than theological or sociological arguments. The church becomes the servant people of God, those who actively take part in the mission of Jesus. Servanthood to God does not mean attaching ourselves to what appears beautiful in the world. The church lives in servanthood that intrudes where sometimes it is not welcomed or desired. It brings God's active love into the most ugly events found in humanity. The church will intrude into such horrible sufferings as death, war, famine, crime, and so forth.

Jesus, the model of honesty, spoke of the first step to acquire truth. He said, "Very truly, I tell you, no one can see the kingdom of God without being born from above," being "born anew"

(John 3:3, see NRSV note). The acquisition of truth occurs only through the born-from-above experience that revolutionizes the sinner into an instrument of God. God's purpose is to bring hope to birth in lives that are being destroyed. He intends to birth hope in people who are degraded by sin and circumstances. God searches with love for the ugly of the world to make them beautiful in him.

Jesus molded the identity of the church of God in his ministry. He saw the church not just as an earthly organization. Instead, it is a living, breathing organism of people who are set apart from sin and gathered together to live in the holiness and love of God. This true church can only be understood through spirituality granted by the work of the Holy Spirit. The believer is expected as a steward of the kingdom of God to live in joyful anticipation of the kingdom being fulfilled among all people on earth. That fulfillment is already partly experienced in the delicious encounter with the tasty fruit of the Spirit (2 Cor. 1:22; 5:5). This is an advance installment of what God has in store for Christians.

The servants of Christ gladly serve their Lord and will even sacrifice their personal comfort to carry out their stewardship responsibility before God. They will not run or hide from the wolf. They will violently, sinlessly, and offensively attack evil under the leadership of the Holy Spirit. They will not falter from the quest for God and his kingdom to fully come among people on earth, as the Lord's Prayer reminds us (Matt. 6:10).

Today's church must stand against evil and seek a restored church without spot or blemish. It must bear good fruit in its stand against evil. The church must venture out of its comfortable club and its hallowed halls to meet humankind in its filth and shame. It must venture into the gutters of human refuge to seek and save the lost (Luke 19:10).

Jesus warns the disciples that wolves will attack the church. There is in our universe an absolute moral and ethical standard. This standard has been revealed only in Jesus Christ. Just as he has given himself to us, we must also give ourselves to him. We guard his church by divine appointment against all forms of evil and sin. Human nature is constantly conceiving evil. All human activities not controlled by the Holy Spirit are tainted by evil. As the church evaluates the warnings of Jesus and puts his teachings into practice against the intrusion of evil, believers will grow in understanding of the ultimate purpose of God.

The redemption of human beings in conflict can only be taken seriously when we are influenced by the presence of Christ and obey his teachings. Jesus was challenging his disciples to guard the flock through personal servanthood. In Mark 12:1-12 Jesus shared a parable of servanthood's relationship to personal ambition and material acquisition. He showed how wrong it is to try to use the gospel for personal gain. Servants are to surrender their life for the Master's work in the vineyard.

When church people quit being merely sideline spectators of grace and become stewards, they discover that they do not own the gospel. Instead, they are responsible for being caretakers of it in the lives of people. Believers can counter the attacks of enemies upon the church only in the will of God and through honest stewardship. Jesus was asking the disciples to be more than just students of him. They were to become servant leaders by demonstrating active servanthood. They were to become servant leaders who would oversee the church and thus be effective against the attacks of evil persons and doctrines.

If servants care for the Master's vineyard and possess a willingness to suffer, they will be blessed by the Master. In this, they receive honor from the Master. They are convinced that their Master is right in what he does, and they will prevail in what the Master desires. As the church awaits the consummation of the kingdom of God on earth, it will be preparing the world for the coming of Christ. The church is to be found pure when the Master returns. As they imitate God's perfect love, these servants will change the world.

Such love is not preserved in some isolated setting apart

from human contact. It is not an escape from earthly responsibilities. It is an offensive, challenging all evil. Servant leaders, therefore, are not freewheeling in what they allow to influence the church. They adhere to value-control management of the church, as responsible stewards of the things that have been entrusted to them. If steward leaders are to be transformational in their work against the wolves, then moral integrity must prevail in all actions of life.

A few years ago, two congregations attempted to join their fellowships together into one church. The two belonged to the same denomination, which was in the middle of a major debate over the inspiration and authority of Scripture. One of the congregations strongly endorsed an evangelical definition of inspiration, while the other congregation strongly opposed it. When the congregation that opposed it could no longer keep their church doors open, they approached the other church about merging the congregations. The evangelical elders did not want anyone to go without the opportunity to worship. They joined together.

The evangelical leaders soon found themselves faced with a problem. The members who had merged with them were promoting their own doctrine. The evangelical elders made a difficult decision, to ask the nonevangelical members to leave the fellowship. It would have been wiser never to have allowed the merger to occur in the first place.

Church people often are more interested in being nice and helpful to others than wise. Yet we are always accountable for our actions. Light and darkness do not spiritually mix. The church must guard against spiritual darkness. There are many actions false leaders use to devour the pure flock of God, actions similar to the tactics of a wolf trying to devour the shepherd's flock. God has given us scriptural safeguards to protect us and to help us defend the faith.

Paul and the Struggle Against Evil Forces

While writing to churches, the apostle Paul presents a number of warnings against the intrusion of evil. Paul is convinced that evil must never be allowed to remain unchallenged.

> Finally, be strong in the Lord and in the strength of his power. Put on the whole armor of God, so that you may be able to stand against the wiles of the devil. For our struggle is not against enemies of blood and flesh, but against the rulers, against the authorities, against the cosmic powers of this present darkness, against the spiritual forces of evil in the heavenly places. (Eph. 6:10-12)

The apostle calls us to stand against the devil's schemes. The devil is our enemy. The church has been called to fight. It is not called to lose the battle, but to win. The Lamb's war is raging against powerful enemies. This is no time for the church to be absorbed simply in itself. The war is killing people spiritually and eternally. The implication of standing means that we put our lives solidly behind the mission entrusted to us. The weapons of our warfare come with divine power to destroy evil strongholds and bring about obedience to Christ (2 Cor. 10:3-6).

Thousands of congregations are stalemated by apathy, self-centeredness, and so forth. The Lamb is fighting a war, and we are to stand with him. Paul calls us to awaken from our spiritual slumber and stand as leaders of purpose and destiny. Yes, there will be trials to face. So what! We have orders to stand firm. God expects obedience of the stewards of the kingdom of God.

Paul Warns the Church at Rome

Paul's letter to the Romans tells us that there will be attempts to disrupt the church's mission. The church is to take note of those who bring division. In Romans 16:17-20 he says,

> I urge you, brothers and sisters, to keep an eye on those who cause dissensions and offenses, in opposition to the

teaching that you have learned; avoid them. For such
people do not serve our Lord Christ, but their own
appetites, and by smooth talk and flattery they deceive the
hearts of the simple-minded. . . . Be wise in what is good and
guileless in what is evil. The God of peace will shortly crush
Satan under your feet."

The church at Rome is not to be deceived. They are to be
spiritually sober, recognizing who among them is demonstrating the love and greatness of Christ, and who is not! Some in the
Roman church will cause disruption. Sometimes the question
arises in local churches regarding what is to be done with a
brother or sister who continually causes division. The answer is
found in the Lord's personal instructions of Matthew 18:15-20.
Paul also tells us that when this form of conflict resolution fails,
then the body of Christ is to have nothing to do with those who
cause division. This is excommunication.

Biblically, excommunication consists of two things. First, it is
the separating of unrepentant sinners from the company of the
righteous of the Lord, giving sinners what they have chosen by
their deeds and words. The sinner looses all rights to the glorious fellowship of Christ. Second, the church in unity turns the
sinner's flesh over to Satan's destruction (1 Cor. 5:1-5). It is the
decision of the church to remove the person from God's protec-
tion for a time and allow the person to feel the weight of sinful
actions, even if it brings bodily ill health.

However, in this final step of Matthew 18:15-20 and in Paul's
words of instruction, the goal is not final destruction of the enemies of the church. Instead, the goal is to bring them to repentance and restoration through discipline (cf. 2 Pet. 3:9). Just because a person has been part of a local church for a long time
does not qualify them to be granted absolute say-so in the business of the church or allow them to behave in such a way that it
is hurtful to others. Paul says that some will give great sermons.
He says some will do nice things for others. Some will look good

on the outside and yet are filled with hearts of wickedness. They serve only themselves.

Paul is deeply concerned that the church recognize those who are dangerous to the church. He wants the church to look ahead and see the potential of the divisive persons' false teaching and conduct. Dedicated members are to do so before these enemies have opportunity to spread their lies as a cancer attacking the body.

The division that they will cause is grievous and burdensome to the entire church. Congregational division will keep the people of God from focusing themselves exclusively upon the mission of outreach into all the world. Division and offense can cause the brothers and sisters to fall short of God's intention for their lives. Therefore, Paul says, keep an eye on those who cause dissensions and offenses; have nothing to do with them. The church collectively is not to embrace these enemies or their falsehood. The church is not to fellowship with them. The reason for this excommunication is because they have refused to obey the Lord Jesus Christ.

Paul Warns the Church at Ephesus

When Paul arrived in Ephesus for the last time, he called the elders of the church to gather and hear his final instructions. In Acts 20:29 he says, "I know that after I have gone, savage wolves will come in among you, not sparing the flock. Some even from your own group will come distorting the truth in order to entice the disciples to follow them. Therefore be alert."

Paul knows by the Lord's own word that the church will be under attack. He knows by personal experience in his ministry with many churches that there will be violent attacks against the church. His pastoral heart cries out to his friends that they would not be deceived. In this he makes known that the dissension and division they are to face will come from those already in the Ephesian fellowship.

These wolves will be grievous to the church because they

will come from within the church. They will speak grievous things. They will be perverted in their speech and draw disciples after themselves. They will not spare the flock. Paul orders the elders at Ephesus to keep watch and to remember his warning to them. They are to remember his burden and tears.

What a shame it is to a congregation that has walked in the light of God if some of the members are disobedient and walk in sin! Even in the disaster of such a crisis, the Lord's instruction for dealing with this issue begins with Matthew 18. The final goal is not excommunication, but rather restoration. Unfortunately, excommunication may have to be exercised as a discipline of the church against its own who are loved by the body of Christ and appear in the family of God. In such times, the heart breaks for the salvation of loved ones. Prayers are unceasingly delivered toward heaven. Tears flow into rivers whose currents are strong, turbulent, and deep.

Somewhere there is a small church with a rich heritage. The previous generation had a great love for the Lord Jesus Christ. Then a new generation arose within the church. They did not confess the Lord Jesus. They did not live in the power and hope of his resurrection. Those presently in the congregation who want to grow spiritually are in constant battle with leadership and others who fear being labeled "fanatical." The apostle John wrote that when a church loses its first love, then it is only fit to be spit out. It has nothing to offer to any soul (Rev. 2:1-7). John cried out for such a church to repent and reclaim their first love for the Lord or face death as a congregation.

Many congregations close their doors due to lack of spiritual vitality. They quit being the church because they are not in Christ. The church at Ephesus received a warning from the apostle John that they had lost their first love. The apostle Paul wrote to the Ephesians to put on the whole armor of God that they might be able to stand against the wiles of the devil (Eph. 6:10-17).

Perhaps the Ephesian believers didn't take the warning of

the apostles seriously enough. Perhaps they forgot that for three years Paul had continuously told them to be watchful. Perhaps they forgot the warnings of Peter and Apollos as they ministered in Ephesus. Perhaps they forgot how to be tough-minded about their faith. No one truly knows what happened in Ephesus. But whatever happened, it is almost certain that much of the ruin came from inside the church. They became spiritual wimps with no backbone to stand spiritually with Christ.

Paul Warns Timothy and Titus

The ministry of Timothy the evangelist had taken him to many parts of the ancient world. The apostle Paul wrote to him, warning him about what was occurring against the early church: "Now the Spirit expressly says that in later times some will renounce the faith by paying attention to deceitful spirits and teachings of demons, through the hypocrisy of liars whose consciences are seared with a hot iron" (1 Tim. 4:1-2).

Paul is determined to let Timothy know that there are dangers coming against the churches. It is a warning concerning apostasy. Although the warning is written for a future event, the context of the letter also alerts the church at that moment to be aware of the danger presently at hand.

Timothy is instructed to remember the gift that he has received through the laying on of hands (1 Tim. 4:14; 2 Tim. 1:6). He is to exercise this gifting for the benefit of the entire church. Timothy has the task of nourishing the church through personal faith and sound teaching. His teaching is to build a strong church totally devoted to Jesus Christ. It is not to be a wishy-washy institution, flowing with the winds of the doctrines and philosophies of men.

Paul says, "Pay close attention to yourself and to your teaching; continue in these things, for in doing this you will save both yourself and your hearers" (1 Tim. 4:16). Timothy is to read the Scriptures publicly, exhort, and explain correct doctrine in order to safeguard the purity of every congregation he comes in contact with in ministry. He is to warn the church everywhere of the apostasies of the day (4:11-16).

In Paul's second letter to Timothy, he warns him of false teachers who will entice the church. In the apostasy that Paul predicts, people will seek false teachers who lie and flatter them. They will not endure sound biblical teaching. They will be wicked people and impostors, deceiving many about the faith (2 Tim. 3:13). They will have a form of godliness, but deny the power of the gospel (3:5).

The letter to Titus says, "Avoid . . . dissensions. . . . After a first and second admonition, have nothing more to do with anyone who causes divisions, since you know that such a person is perverted and sinful, being self-condemned" (Titus 3:9-11).

In the days of Paul and his successors, in our time, and in the future, the battle facing the church is pitted between the power of God and satanic influences found in the world. The church is commissioned to "hold to the standard of sound teaching that you have heard from me, in the faith and love that are in Christ Jesus" (2 Tim. 1:13).

Paul Warns the Church at Colossae

Paul and Timothy jointly wrote a letter to the Colossian church to help the believers remain in the truth of Jesus Christ. They warn the church to "see to it that no one takes you captive through philosophy and empty deceit, according to human tradition, according to the elemental spirits of the universe, and not according to Christ" (Col. 2:8). The theme of the letter is that Christ is supreme in all things (1:15-20). Yet, even though Christ is supreme, he places his church on alert against the intrusions of human philosophies.

The glorious church of Christ is to exist in his power and fullness. Members are to seek only those things found in heaven with Christ (Col. 3:2). They are not to be caught up in worship of angels (2:18), self-imposed regulations (2:20-23), or the arrogance of the world's governing powers (2:15). They are to be clothed with the new self and "with love, which binds everything together in perfect harmony. And let the peace of Christ rule in your hearts, to which indeed you were called in the one body" (3:14-15).

They are not to be stupid in what they do on earth. They are to be wise, innocent, standing firm in the power of Jesus Christ, having true Christian lives, being thankful, and doing everything in the name of the Lord Jesus (3:1-25). Sometimes well-meaning Christians claim they are happy to be fools for Christ (1 Cor. 4:10). They have taken this phrase and twisted it around to make it say something it was never intended to mean. Let all the church of the living God be wise unto the Lord and demonstrators of his power!

The Warning of Hebrews

The writer of Hebrews declares the great everlasting truth of Jesus Christ: "Jesus Christ is the same yesterday and today and forever. Do not be carried away by all kinds of strange teachings; for it is well for the heart to be strengthened by grace, not by regulations about food, which have not benefited those who observe them" (Heb. 13:8-9).

Jesus Christ is superior to all human wisdom. His wisdom establishes the church by grace. In his loving grace, he urges his truth to be known and warns the church to stay away from strange doctrines.

Hebrews also urges us to "hold fast to the confession of our hope without wavering," to meet together regularly, and to encourage each other (10:23-25). Those who willfully persist in sin face God's judgment (10:26-31). The author warns of the danger of backsliding and the effect it can have on others: "See to it that no one fails to obtain the grace of God; that no root of bitterness springs up and causes trouble, and through it many become defiled" (12:15).

Other New Testament Counsel on Conflict

The New Testament is full of teachings regarding evil's intru-sions into the life of the church. God has commissioned the church to be on guard against the enemies of God. All Christians are to fully understand what we believe, and live our lives under the guidance of the Holy Spirit. In conflict resolution it is essen-tial to know that the attacks upon the character of the church are satanic in nature.

Our war is not with people but with false doctrines and vari-ous forms of evil. When we recognize the satanic element in conflict, it frees us by guarding us against violating our human opponents on any issue. It gives us motivation to seek their spiri-tual well-being by releasing the gospel to confront their lives. It frees us from evil actions against them and allows us to dialogue in our own truthful integrity. The opponents that we face will not be helped with deadly assaults, but rather with love.

Love is not spineless. Love seeks the ultimate good of others without losing our own integrity. The conflicts between persons will cease through a demonstration of the love of Christ for each other. This does not mean that we water down the message of the gospel. It cannot be diluted. The gospel presents an absolute ethic in the universe. Love does mean that all in the church must put the concerns of Christ before everything else in life.

The church in America needs a massive movement toward Christlikeness. Many churches have uncritically adapted to the prevailing culture more than to the Christian faith. Too many Christians will tell you that they love Christ, but they cannot ex-plain what is unique about their love. This is dangerous to the church. False leaders will infiltrate congregations that cannot de-fine what their Christian faith means to them, and how faith must confront culture to finish what God the Father has pur-posed to do in the world. Christianity is not a faith declaring that life will always go smoothly. It is a faith that, in the midst of the battles of life, calls for developing spiritual backbone and spiritu-al formation.

The church is no less than the body of Christ spiritually united with God. Leadership in the church is leadership involved with service to God. Conflict resolution must be spiritually founded, ethically conducted, and thoughtfully received. Conflicts must be handled and processed in a style of serving God, not simply seeking to please others.

The gospel itself has immense personal appeal. Conflict resolution seeks to acquire God's character as presented in Jesus Christ. When God has a message, he sends someone to deliver the message. This is a privilege granted to his servants because he has chosen us to advertise it. We are to take God's love and use it in communicating the need to be restored to God. Our model for handling conflict resolution is to do it with the attitude of Jesus Christ himself (Phil. 2:5-11).

We do not just deliver a verbal warning to those in conflict. We give *ourselves* that they might be restored to God. We give as servants entrusted with great responsibility and eternal knowledge. Our lives are living sacrifices given to God (Rom. 12:1-2). Our message of reconciliation is not just one of feelings and behavior. Even though evil is a seductive influence upon people, the gospel message does not ever agree that God has surrendered creation to the satanic. The message proclaims that God is in absolute control of everything. We have been granted freedom to serve God's plan of redemption, the ultimate overthrow of evil. We are servants who deliver unconditional love to a desolate world that is in stubborn resistance to peace in Christ.

The Kingdom of God in Conflict Resolution
The Kingdom of God on the Offense

There are two spiritual kingdoms in existence. The kingdom of God is opposed by the kingdom of darkness. The apostle Paul wrote to the church at Colossae concerning the redemption of Christ: "He has rescued us from the power of darkness and transferred us into the kingdom of his beloved Son" (Col. 1:13). Severe conflict is occurring between the two kingdoms. The kingdom of God is actively seeking to bring people out of the darkness and to God. Satan's kingdom is violently opposing divine intervention into human lives. The church has been given divine authority to attack the kingdom of darkness and rescue those who have been enslaved by it.

Jesus began his public ministry by preaching that the kingdom of God was at hand. He called everyone to repent and believe the good news (Matt. 4:17; Mark 1:14-15). It has been nearly two thousand years since Jesus made that statement. Jesus was not talking about a geographic location (for the kingdom) but about the reign of God, freshly active in his own ministry. Jesus meant that this kingdom was now presenting itself as a reality to destroy the sinful condition of human beings, to deliver them from bondage to Satan, fear, and evil (Luke 13:16; Heb. 2:15).

This manifestation of the kingdom is possible only in the person of Jesus Christ and his followers who extended his ministry. Jesus brought not so much a defense against the darkness as an *offense* to destroy evil's impact upon humankind. He was delivering those enslaved by "the strong man." Jesus said, "If it is by the Spirit (finger) of God that I cast out demons, then the kingdom of God has come to you" (Matt. 12:27-30; Luke 11:20). The kingdom has come! May it come more fully! (Matt. 6:10). Christ has brought emancipation from darkness for those enslaved in the satanic kingdom. He puts believers into the new creation (2 Cor. 5:17; Col. 1:13).

The overthrow of demonic domination in the lives of people is still provoking violent opposition. The reign of God is offensive: it demands of all who encounter the gospel an obedient yes to its demands or a rebellious no. The choice is clear. We may choose either God and his freeing reign, or Satan and his destructive bondage. At its core, peacemaking offers people the opportunity and responsibility to grasp the truth of spiritual freedom through Jesus Christ. If this does not occur, there can be no true peace.

The Glorious Triumph of the Kingdom of God

God's reign is not only for the present age but for the future, too. The church is living in the tension of anticipating the consummation of the kingdom. Christ is now progressively putting all things under his rule. Yet the church waits for the consummation of the kingdom on earth. Already, the values of the kingdom of God are impacting the world's order of values. This has produced tremendous conflict as darkness gives way to light.

The old age of evil pulls upon believers and the church. But we have pledged obedience to the new age of God's reign. We live in the overlap and battlefield of the two ages, old and new. As Paul says, "The ends of the ages have come upon us" (1 Cor. 10:11). We are the "children of the kingdom" (Matt. 13:38), part of Christ's victory as he overcomes Satan and evil (Luke 10:17-18; John 12:31; Rev. 12:7-12) and rescues more and more people. Paul warns us to persevere in testing and temptation, depending on God's faithfulness (1 Cor. 10).

In church discord, one of the greatest hurdles to overcoming conflict is the development of a congregational attitude that God is winning the battle. It is far easier to look at what our human eyes see—the bleakness, which we do need to recognize. Yet beyond and above that, we need to look in faith for the victory of Jesus Christ to be consummated in our daily lives and in his triumph over all evil powers (1 Cor. 15:24-28).

Conflicts to Be Conquered by the Kingdom

The apostle Paul wrote to the Christians at Galatia, "When the fullness of time had come, God sent his Son, born of a woman, born under the law, in order to redeem those who were under the law, so that we might receive adoption as children" (Gal. 4:4-5). The meaning of history has been revealed through Jesus Christ. History itself is meaningless without this connection with Christ.

The constant of all history is God's sovereign call through Christ, and human response to him. The kingdom of God exists both in the present and the future. The present and the future are linked together. Time is the place where God and his creatures interact together. There are always new things happening in time. Time progressively moves forward. It is moving toward the coming (Greek: *parousia*) of Christ, when he will put all things in subjection to him (1 Cor. 15:23-28). Therefore, the kingdom is the future age impinging on and overcoming the present age. The triumph of God's reign is coming.

In addition to the historical dimension of the kingdom, there is also a moral dimension. Human nature is sinful. The sinfulness extends to all human activities in this age. Our best intentions are tainted by sin and the fallen world in which we live. Whenever conflict resolution merely uses human engineers, it is deficient. Human sinfulness affects everything we are determined to accomplish.

Biblical conflict resolution is an integration with the sovereignty of God. We seek divine holiness to resolve sinful conditions. All human history is moving toward the judgment of God. Peacemakers must never forget, in the universal perspective of the kingdom of God, that sin is to be done away with forever. This God has decreed, and this we firmly believe. We wait for the future fullness of the kingdom of God. Meanwhile, God's reign is resolving conflict; we must see Christ working to fulfill his will to save us from our sins. When we have conflict with others in the church, we must have spiritual vision and desire their full salvation by Jesus Christ. Then and only then are we seeing with the eyes of Jesus.

Christ's kingdom will conquer all conflict aimed against its standards and dominion. The pain of the present conflicts of life will be overcome by the beauty of the eternal sovereignty of God. The creation is still groaning for the day of consummation (Rom. 8:18-25). Yet in the timing of God, all the groanings will cease in the presence of Christ.

Can all conflict be resolved in this present age? The answer is no! Not until every tongue confesses that Jesus Christ is Lord

(Phil. 2:11). That is our hope and prayer. When that happens, then the old has passed away, and the new has come, purged of sin and pain, with healing for the nations (Rev. 21–22). The Prince of Peace must set up his kingdom of peace on earth just as God presently reigns in peace in heaven (Matt. 6:10).

Summary

In ministry, the peacemaker must be aware of two major levels of conflict. The first level involves disagreements between Christian believers. This is called internal conflict resolution. The second level involves conflict faced by Christians who are deliberately persecuted for their faith. The role of negotiating peace on this level is called eternal conflict resolution.

The early church did not exist in a totally peaceful environment. It was constantly pressed to prove its integrity to the world. The church knew that it could expect both internal and external conflict. Jesus, Paul, and other New Testament leaders warned of threats to the church. They described types of problems that would appear in the life of the people of God. They taught leaders how to comprehend what was godly truth in contrast to the often-disguised evil presented by the powers of darkness in the world.

The kingdom of God is always powerfully opposed to the kingdom of darkness. Jesus commanded the disciples of the Lord to bear good fruit to prove their discipleship. In peacemaking, the ministry of conflict resolution calls for more than human ability if we are to bear good fruit and succeed spiritually. It incorporates the greatness of the grace of God in reconciling people unto himself. Peacemaking ministry summons the would-be peacemaker to acquire a personal and life-transforming vision of God reconciling the world to himself, and to see our part in the plan of God.

There is a bonding between God and his servants that mandates a lifestyle of servanthood before God. The church is appointed by God to be an organism of holy servants permanently attached to God. This servanthood is a commitment to a heavenly cause. Servant leaders are given the authority and power of Almighty God to invade sinful human darkness.

The servants of God react to their encounters with evil both intelligently and in dependence upon God. They imitate the love of God and hold it as their standard. They are neither apathetic nor spineless in how they relate to evil. The battle of the servants of God is not with people, but with forms of evil that destroy the lives of persons. The battle involves more than verbal rebukes against evil. We need to give ourselves in servanthood to restore others to God. This is no easy task. The kingdom of God and the kingdom of darkness are forcefully opposed to each other.

God is winning the battle. The church too often perceives the battle as being lost. It is not! The final triumph of God's reign over history will yet occur. Christ's kingdom will conquer all conflict aimed against its standards and dominion.

CHAPTER FOUR

When Peace Is Not Sought by Others

No Pat Answers in Conflict Resolution

Sooner or later, we wonder what to do as peacemakers when we have failed in producing peace in the church. We have diligently sought God for solutions to problems and consistently followed the teachings of the New Testament. So what can be done when it appears that all our efforts seem fruitless?

Pat answers may develop in a small-group study or in a Sunday school lesson. Often well-meaning people come to the false conclusion that when we have tried our best and the other person has remained hostile toward us, then the problem is no longer ours but theirs. I have never been comfortable with this idea. It is deficient in several ways.

First, *love for the gospel* should compel us to desire restored fellowship, not to compromise, retreat, or surrender our ministry in Christ. The gospel itself is good news about restoration to God (Jer. 3:22; 2 Cor. 5:17-18; Eph. 2:16; Col. 1:21-22; Heb. 2:17; Gal. 6:1; Isa. 57:18). The real question becomes this: can we love those who are hostile toward us, and seek their well-being?

With great wisdom, God has placed each of us in a particular setting of time and place where we are surrounded by our enemies (Ps. 23:5). The Lord not only refuses to remove those adversaries from our lives; he insists that his reign and love will not be forced into spiritual retreat by their distaste for our allegiance to God. Sin has ruined many lives. Our battles as peacemakers are not meant to destroy people, but rather to establish love in them with the same enthusiasm that God has in loving us.

Jesus spoke about loving our enemies (Matt. 5:44; Luke 6:27). How can we love our enemies if we are isolated from them? How can we love our enemies if we have abandoned them in their greatest hour, at the place of their greatest need? Sometimes the idea of loving those who hate us is irritating to our spiritual mind-set until we are confronted with the living presence of Jesus Christ. We learn in Christ to spiritually intercede for them with tears; our spirits are so often filled with empathy for the pain of our enemies. The Holy Spirit, desiring salvation for them, will intercede by awakening us to a new awareness. We all need the hope that only the Spirit can provide for our lives.

We learn that we have no part in the kingdom of God apart from his love. God's love places us in the midst of our enemies. His love drives us to seek reconciliation for and with others even when our attempts at reconciliation fail. We may experience personal exhaustion from our involvement in the tragedies of others who need God's salvation, but God's love is still working. Reconciliation is more than people settling differences. It is also a covenant between people and God, a bonding into true spirituality by Christ. We are driven to share the same love we have received.

Love is an active response to God's graciousness to us. The Scriptures are full of mandates to intervene in the lives of others, such as the following:

> My friends, if anyone is detected in a transgression, you who have received the Spirit should restore such a one in a spirit of gentleness. Take care that you yourselves are not tempted. Bear one another's burdens, and in this way you will fulfill the law of Christ. (Gal. 6:1-2)

> As God's chosen ones, holy and beloved, clothe yourselves with compassion, kindness, humility, meekness, and patience. Bear with one another and, if anyone has a complaint

against another, forgive each other; just as the Lord has
forgiven you, so you also must forgive. (Col. 3:12-13)

Even if someone refuses to make peace with us, we are required
by God to forgive them with love. This refusal to be reconciled
does not wipe out our responsibility toward them. We may experience rejection consistently by them for years. Love doesn't
give up (1 Cor. 13:4-8).

The apostle James says,

My brothers and sisters, if anyone among you wanders
from the truth and is brought back by another, you should
know that whoever brings back a sinner from wandering
will save the sinner's soul from death and will cover a
multitude of sins. (James 5:19-20)

Notice what Paul says: "We urge you, beloved, to admonish
the idlers, encourage the faint hearted, help the weak, be patient
with all of them" (1 Thess. 5:14). God's love is experienced in his
compassion for us. Our love is brought to life in the lives of
others by the same type of compassion.

Such compassion is not a wimpy attempt to influence others.
It is the engineering of God's love in our lives as peacemakers.
Thus we have an intensity of concern for others that goes beyond lip service to deliberate action for our enemies' spiritual
well-being. When this is not accomplished, we may well see our
neighbor depart into eternal damnation, alienated from Christ.
Such thoughts of them being apart from Christ ought to bruise
any restraining pride in our lives that allows us to be idle when
they are fading away into eternity, lost. By grace we have been
saved (Eph. 2:8). By grace they may be saved, too.

We ought to plead for their souls in prayers, fastings, and
personal words and actions. Love means going the second, third,
and fourth mile beyond our normal routines to seek their spiritual and physical good. It means forgiving as Jesus taught us,
seventy times seven, then keeping no records of wrongdoings

(Matt. 18:22). It is not our rights that we claim in reconciliation. It is a gut-wrenching love for our enemies that we relentlessly pursue.

Jesus put it this way:

> For I was hungry and you gave me food, I was thirsty and you gave me something to drink, I was a stranger and you welcomed me, I was naked and you gave me clothing. I was sick and you took care of me, I was in prison and you visited me. (Matt. 25:35-36)

The only pat answer acceptable in conflict resolution is the personal involvement of the believer in the actions of love. We must persist in our belief that love will triumph in our personal lives and affect others.

That plan of action will not always be understood. Others will respond to love either negatively or positively. The actions of love lead us to an eternity of blessings with God. Faith motivates us to push into the unknown regions of life that seem uncomfortable, to be reconciled with our brothers and sisters. We travel the road with scriptural directions to solve the problems. We navigate by the guidance and power of the Holy Spirit to work his plan out in our lives. By faith we travel unknown roads to seek the straying and disgruntled. We travel as fallible people who are receiving God's love and depending on God's love and grace working in us.

Second, *desire for obedience* follows our love for the gospel in urging us to continue peacemaking even in difficult situations. Most types of pat answers are deficient because they too often are excuses for not obeying the Scriptures and especially Matthew 18:15-20. Do we really believe that if we search the mind of God with all our heart and strength, we will find answers to all our conflicts? Do we really want answers to our problems? Or are we just playing a deadly game to promote our own agenda in a battle with someone else?

Our excuses that prevent restored fellowship in the church

may send someone to hell. Can there be a more sobering thought in the Christian life? The greatest problem most Christians face in conflict resolution is their own unwillingness to seek spiritual guidance and to wait upon the Lord for his counsel.

Jesus said, "But strive first for the kingdom of God and his righteousness, and all these things will be given to you as well" (Matt. 6:33). The precious promises of the kingdom of God are given to us. They are conditioned, however, on our seeking the reality of the kingdom above everything else that filters into our lives. The pat answers that we devise to solve our problems are useless for spiritual success unless they are founded upon the counsel of God. Searching for God's will and wisdom in any crisis is not a vain activity of the mind. Intense spiritual searching reveals the hidden things of the heart that destroy the reign of love in our lives. Hence, we need to set aside blocks of daily time to meet intentionally with God in prayer.

God insists that we search for him in every part of our lives. This search does not mean that in times of crisis we automatically receive answers to our deepest concerns. Some problems are complex, and we lack understanding; so they may take years to solve. Yet we must persist before God until the bounty found in prayer is realized in God's response and direction.

Someone once said, "God is never behind time, or ahead of time. He is always on time." It may take days, weeks, and years for us to engage in spiritually searching for God regarding the complex issues that pester us. As we do this, we will begin to realize that the time of waiting for God to act is not wasted. In the hands of God, we learn of his mercy for us. We discover that he is carefully at work in the lives of others, wanting to make known to them that they too can receive his great salvation.

Sometimes we are too active to fulfill God's plans for us to serve him. We race ahead at full speed, rather than discovering his intentions for us. Often we fail to walk by the leadings of his Spirit because we are spiritually insensitive and overly busy.

How can we experience the depths of Christ's love if we refuse to move toward deep fellowship with Christ? There are too many believers who are spiritually lazy and deceived by the ways of the world. We must be spiritually changed to be emancipated from the bondage of sin and from our own personal self-deception about our importance in the universe.

The prophet Ezekiel in the sixth century B.C. was called to abandon lazy and pathetic habits and plead for the salvation of Israel. God's call upon him was so demanding that he realized he was accountable for what he would or would not do for the people of Israel. The Lord told him,

> Mortal, I have made you a sentinel for the house of Israel;
> whenever you hear a word from my mouth, you shall give
> them warning from me. If I say to the wicked, "You shall
> surely die," and you give them no warning, or speak to
> warn the wicked from their wicked way, in order to save
> their life, those wicked persons shall die for their iniquity;
> but their blood I will require at your hand. (Ezek. 3:17-18)

Confronting sin is a serious matter because all people are valuable. Sin destroys life. We work on conflict resolution to restore the life God intended for people to live. Pat answers can kill souls and leave them eternally in sin and separated from God. Spiritual watchers may not always be popular among the masses of humanity. But in God's plan of reconciliation, such sentinels are necessary for restoring lives and freeing them from sin. The peacemaker is the carrier of the good news of God's restoring love.

Third, we are *called to rescue the perishing*. Most pat answers keep the church from engaging in spiritual warfare against the enemy of our souls. We rationalize that our responses in rescuing the lost are sometimes good, but somehow we have been deceived. We have believed a lie, that we should play it safe by remaining in our personal comfort zones and avoiding our enemies. We like being in a place that feels secure, where we can call the shots. Such a comfort zone prevents change and mobility in Christ; it is a dangerous pit of destruction.

Western culture is being destroyed by an apathetic church. Members are absorbed with seeking their own personal comfort rather than being open to self-sacrifice. However, the church has a responsibility for moral leadership in society, to be a sentinel, speaking and acting against sin and for the truth. If the church fails to be that moral watchdog, then all that is left is the state's code of conduct, which often falls far short of the gospel. The church is called to battle against the lies and intrusions of the satanic. It can be salt and light in the world and thus help to work against the moral collapse of society (Matt. 5:13-16).

The primary goal of the church is the salvation of every human being in the world. Pat answers persuade us not to be involved in human hurts and moral accountability; this cripples the outreach of the church. Yes, we are all people in pain; but let us arise above the fears and pains found commonly among all people. Let us be found obediently engaged in joyous and active servanthood to Christ, resisting society's evils. It is a rare saint who will say, "Lord, I am totally available to you, and I am willing to suffer." We need more of these incredible people.

In writing to the Corinthians, the apostle Paul tells them, "The weapons of our warfare are not merely human, but they have divine power to destroy strongholds. We destroy arguments and every proud obstacle raised up against the knowledge of God, and we take every thought captive to obey Christ" (2 Cor. 10:4-5). We do not use carnal weapons to wage physical war. Carnal weapons destroy us and others. Paul says our weapons are spiritual and consequently more powerful than the strongholds of Satan. We can prevail unto victory in the power of Jesus Christ and his resurrection.

Finally, by clinging to pat answers, we disobey God. If we see a sister or brother in sin, we must do something about it that will promote their reconciliation to the Lord and fellow members. So often Christians are afraid to speak spiritual words to those in need of salvation. They are afraid of being misunderstood or disliked. They falsely believe that it is the preacher's responsibility, not their own. But if we don't speak, they may die in their sins. But if we do bring back a sinner, we "will save the sinner's soul from death and will cover a multitude of sins" (James 5:19-20).

There are several requirements for peacemaking: the practice of spiritual brokenness before the Lord, making ourselves available for God's plan to work in our lives, and following the procedures of Matthew 18.

Hard Questions About Involvement in Conflict

There are many questions peacemakers may ask themselves to help them understand their own role in conflict resolution.

One pastor, after a turbulent first year in a congregation, sat down one day and wrote out a list of sins that he was aware of in his congregation: usage of foul language, homosexual practices with a man dressing as a woman, drug usage, alcoholism, incest, divorce, adultery, prejudice, slander, backbiting, gossiping, criticizing and hating others, lack of trust and forgiveness, lying, physical abuse of spouses, and materialism. When he had completed his list, he felt emotionally overwhelmed.

Then he asked himself, "Have I been called to pastor Sodom and Gomorrah?" He remarked, "I dread the brimstone of judgment. I just cannot understand how so many people can claim Christ and yet live such wicked lives."

The questions we ask in the midst of difficulty as church leaders and as peacemakers can be overwhelming. However, they are extremely important to help us decipher the directions we must follow to bring peace in the church. Here is a sampling of questions that peacemakers may find themselves asking about crises in the congregations where they serve. There are no simple answers to questions like these because the questions themselves arise from a cry of the human soul seeking hope in times of despair.

1. What is the history of the church that led to the crisis being experienced today? How did sin first take root in the congregation?
2. What does a truly spiritual church look like, emotionally and socially? Is there spirituality in the church, and what does it look like? What will peace look like when it is accomplished?
3. What do I do when I have inherited a church mess (conflict) from the previous pastor?
4. How can I trust people who one moment are hot and the next moment cold toward me? How do I love them with wisdom? How do I guard my backside and be open to their needs and confusions?
5. How can I as a peacemaker release myself enough from church-related problems to help me maintain good mental health and a positive outlook on life?
6. What must I do to keep myself from becoming bitter when conflict is directed toward me? How can I overcome personal persecution that is extremely hurtful? How can I assist the church toward healing when I am the focus of the issues at hand?
7. Why can't people love each other in the church?
8. What does a peacemaker do when there are people in a congregation who are deliberately trying to destroy others?
9. How far is too far in negotiating a solution to a crisis in the church? When is it better to let the crisis continue so that the real issues may be addressed?
10. How does one bring people together in a congregation where over the years the antagonists have teamed up together in groups and each group now plays an important role in the church's checks and balances? How does one get them to love each other?
11. Is there a witness of Christian love in my church?
12. What is the difference between going to church and *being* the church?
13. Have I become a peacemaker who is pressed down so far that it is now impossible for me to be genuine? Do I

have a human right to be myself despite what others
would like to promote in me?

14. What are the primary issues in the church? What are the
    secondary issues in the church?
15. Is it sometimes necessary to push people out of the
    congregation for the sake of the whole church? Is this a
    biblical solution?
16. Do I need to seek forgiveness of others?
17. Does the church need outside help from denomination-
    al leaders? Can they really help us? What will they think
    of me, and how will it affect my future in the denomina-
    tion?
18. In my efforts, am I seeking first the heart of God, or am I
    just being stubborn in how I do things in the church?
19. Is this church dead? Is it going to die? Can it be revived?
    Do I want to stay in this leadership position if it is going
    to die? Will others think I am a failure because I am un-
    able to find a solution to the problems?
20. When is it time to leave a church as a pastor or lay lead-
    er?
21. How can I as a peacemaker arise above my own prob-
    lems to be a healer for the church?

Peacemaking is not something that happens by the peacemaker just wishing for a solution. We live in a world that is rest-
less and in rebellion against God, and that rebellion has even
swept into the church like "wild waves of the sea" (Jude 8-16).
Achievement of peace has a definite price tag, and it never happens without spiritual labor.

Physical and mental work has its importance in the provi-
dence of God (Gen. 2:15, 20). Spiritual labor, however, involves
participating with heaven in providing solutions to earthly problems. How often have we labored physically, but neglected to labor spiritually in prayer, fastings, and preparation for declaring
of the word of God? Yet it is good news for us that God has chosen weak vessels to be filled with his power in the solving of
conflict (2 Cor. 4:7-15).

God has not chosen as his representatives of peace the highly gifted of this world who respond with haughty pride and personal ambition. He has chosen simple people who are willingly attached to him. These are the people who are walking in childlike faith with God. They have chosen to please him by their faith. They are prepared to wait on him until solutions are found. In their trials, patience is developed through suffering. They have a hope that is not disappointed. They are bonded to the heart of God.

When the questions seem unanswered and the crisis is painful beyond description or imagination, it is comforting to know that God does not forget the simple in faith. He loves their fellowship and agrees with their pure requests. God tears down the enemy's strongholds for the sake of the faithful.

We must never forget that when God answers prayers quickly or gradually, he does so out of love so that we may help others see that God loves them too. What can happen when we obediently submit to God's will in Christ? We find solutions to what we have not understood. All that peacemakers are allowed to claim as their own is the knowledge that Jesus loves them beyond all description. Peacemakers will not be allowed to live surface relationships, separated from others in the congregation. They will be moved into a sphere of fellowship with others, bonded together in the Holy Spirit.

Spiritual leaders who are broken before the Lord must deal with the risk of being personally exposed. In a hostile ministry environment, it takes great faith to be openly vulnerable. Yet we must be vulnerable if others are to see and to experience Jesus Christ in us. Conflict resolution needs godly examples to show the way of love and forgiveness.

James 5:14-16 reminds us to "confess [our] sins to one another, and pray for one another, so that [we] may be healed. The prayer of the righteous is powerful and effective." This does not mean that leaders are to act foolishly, in mere self-assertiveness. Our questions about our own spiritual state should lead to spiritual truth. Spiritual truth should lead to honesty. Honesty should lead us into further illumination by the Holy Spirit and his fellowship. Our fellowship will then become intimacy with God and others who love Christ. This is the core of all unity.

Spiritual Discernment for Doing Right

It was the twenty-fourth day of February, and the congregation was split down the middle in controversy. The pastor had just finished his sermon when two key leaders asked to speak to him privately. In a side room, they raked him over the coals for the next one and a half hours. The church had been divided for some time, and he had been subjected to weekly assault about things for which he had not been responsible in the church.

The pastor was at the breaking point when the new attack occurred. The leaders were calling for a vote to get rid of him. When he finally got home, tears began to flow steadily. He knew he had not caused the problems, and he knew he stood righteously before the Lord. The pastor knew he had done all that he humanly could do in the church.

The pastor and his wife set the following Tuesday aside to search for God's will through prayer and fasting. The number one question for them: "Is it time to leave this pastorate?" They began their deep quest through prayer and the searching of the Scriptures. In John 10 they found strength in the story of the Great Shepherd, who would lead them and not forget their needs. As they prayed and sought God, they asked him to show them what they were doing right in the church.

The pastor had been criticized for poor sermons. As they continued in prayer, they realized that this was not true. He had faithfully proclaimed the word of God. They had pastored elsewhere, and his sermons had been appreciated by other churches. They began to realize that the congregation was in bereavement over the current division among themselves, and some would not receive anything they said. They also knew that some people were being touched by the messages. Mistakes had been made, but their consciences were clear before the Lord. Prayer and openness before God revealed that those who were criticizing had never supported them since their coming to that church.

As the day wore on, the Lord opened their eyes to the real issue. They were convinced that it was not the preaching. Was it catering to certain persons, or competitiveness, or whatever? Their prayers began to seek intensively for a solution to the crisis. They became convinced that there was unacknowledged sin in the congregation. In the search for divine direction, they pondered many conclusions. One of the most important ones was a realization that the pastor and his wife were still relevant to God's work, whether at the present church or another one.

Spiritual searching for the will of God is never wasted time in conflict resolution and management. It is mandatory in times of crisis. All too often, peacemakers and congregations have forsaken the benefits of concentrated prayer with fasting. It takes time with God to help Christians see the real issues at hand and not be fooled by what appear to be the problems.

The pastor and his wife were not the only ones committed to prayer. A number of members backing the pastoral couple also gathered for prayer. In the time of prayer and searching, they all realized the presence of the Lord, speaking to them. God is always willing to intercede when Christians commit themselves wholeheartedly to seek him. The Lord revealed the sins of the church to many of them. They wrote them down.

Several days later the pastor received an affirmative vote. This did not mean the war was over. It was not! God still maintains the right to remove the pastor or to keep him in the church. Pastors do not always see the full results of their labors.

It had been a hard fight, personally draining for both pastor and laity. Fighting is hard when the stakes are high and relate to human sin and eternal life. Wisdom calls for sanctified common sense in our business and constant empowerment by the Holy

Spirit in our lives. Prayer is the vital necessity for Christian advancement in the church. It is personal and corporate. Each individual Christian needs the vehicle of prayer to challenge sin. The entire corporate body of Christ needs prayer to have the mind of Christ in any given situation.

Churches are made up of many people, and consequently they have distinctive personalities. It is good not to be alone in our struggles. This pastor needed the support of others who would search for God's help. In the upper room the Holy Spirit fell upon ordinary people who had gathered together in obedience to Christ. The Spirit fell upon the whole community of believers (Acts 1–2). We have been made for a relationship of intimacy with God. We are not isolated individuals, doing God's work alone. One log on a fire produces little heat. Many logs cause a blazing dynamo of love in service to the Master of the universe. There is no substitute for a searching heart. Concentrated prayer with fasting helps shake off the bondage produced by feeling we are helpless in crises.

Paul and Barnabas knew the value of asking questions and searching for the will of God. Barnabas was the one who befriended Paul after he heard the concerns of the church about his conversion. They both understood the importance of obtaining spiritual wisdom from God. In ministry at Lystra, Iconium, and Antioch they prayed and fasted. As a result, they received godly direction for appointing elders. They asked God for help, and he gave it (Acts 14:21-23).

In ministering at Thessalonica, Paul, Silas, and Timothy prayed night and day to see the congregation again, so they could supply them with what was lacking in their faith (1 Thess. 3:10). God wants us to be persistent in asking him to supply the blessings of heaven for the church. Spiritual wisdom is promised to the church. "If any of you is lacking in wisdom, ask God, who gives to all generously and ungrudgingly, and it will be given you" (James 1:5). Jesus in his message concerning the last days said, "For I will give you words and a wisdom that none of your opponents will be able to withstand or contradict" (Luke 21:15). God has given precious promises so we can obtain wisdom in times of troubles.

Prayers and fastings are necessary ingredients to all successful spiritual people. Does this mean if we pray and fast in the church, we will always agree and have unity? Of course not, but it can be the greatest catalyst ever discovered for spiritual emancipation. Even Barnabas and Paul had their differences. When Barnabas wanted to take John Mark with them, Paul disagreed sharply (Acts 13:13; 15:37-41). Barnabas and Paul separated and were preaching the gospel in different locations, with different co-workers. God still used them. They still loved each other. But they certainly did not agree on everything.

Defending Personal Integrity for the Gospel

According to the apostle Paul, "All who want to live a godly life in Christ Jesus will be persecuted" (2 Tim. 3:12). Anyone who lives a godly life will suffer satanic attacks upon their lives. The godly do suffer, but in their suffering they place their hope in the One who delivers them from despair.

The young pastor sat in my office on a cold winter's day, still overcome by the actions of his church board. He had been desperately trying to do the work of Christ, but he had been misunderstood. The board had given him a written list of his weaknesses. According to them, he had an attitude problem, didn't want to work with them, and did not trust them. He was seen as unbending and refusing to change. They told him that he was unloving and without compassion, self-centered, doing as he pleased.

They claimed he was a dictator, with wrong priorities in use of his time, not able to relate to older adults, not open to correction, and giving the impression of never being wrong. They charged him with lack in visiting the congregation, poor pulpit manners, insensitivity to people, and sharing accusations about others that couldn't be backed up. They said he lacked social graces, had a contentious spirit, lacked involvement with youth, was absent without permission, evaded questions or issues, and was more loyal to other people than to the board.

I do not know how many of these accusations were true. I do know that love does not tear down; instead, it seeks to build up the body of Christ. More is accomplished through love than through all the methodology invented by human beings. Love is the best way. When leaders are condemned for who they are, they lose that part of themselves that allows them to see their personal value. Is it evil to offer "positive criticism" without an atmosphere of love? Perhaps it is the worst form of evil. It is the deliberate attack upon others to destroy them, although acting as though what we are doing is for their own good or for the church's good. Nothing is further from the truth. In such cases, the motivation to encounter each other is not for mutual well-being. It is done in selfishness, a merciless battle to conquer a person's life identity and focus. It is wrong.

The apostle Paul's encounter with the false teachers at Corinth is an excellent example of evil's attempt to destroy what is good and holy.

Accusations Against the Apostle Paul

The false apostles at Corinth attacked Paul's credibility to provide godly leadership ministry within the church. If the accusations of his opponents can be proved correct, then there is good reason to refuse to support Paul's claim of apostleship. If Paul's claim of apostleship is refuted, then his teachings can be considered suspicious. The accusations will not simply disappear. The charges against Paul include the following:

First, Paul is perceived as unreliable and vacillating (1 Cor. 1:12-18). Attacks aimed at him were intended to make him seem foolish and unspiritual in the eyes of the Corinthians. Paul's opponents were saying, "Don't trust the man because he is a scoundrel. He will steer you down a wrong path." Paul cannot afford to sit back comfortably in the distant city of Ephesus and expect the Corinthians to quietly back him up and dismiss the allegations against him. He is forced to be aggressive toward his enemies, to destroy their evil influence upon the church. If peacemaking is to occur, the apostle must prove that he has the integrity to do the task. If the accusations of his enemies can be proved false, his integrity as an apostle is strengthened in the church.

Second, Paul is perceived as being full of pride, boasting of the fact that he is an exceptional apostle of Jesus Christ (2 Cor. 3:1; 4:2; 5:12; 10:13-14).

Third, his opponents are declaring that Paul has been injurious to the congregation. No peacemakers want to harm the body of Christ by what they do in the church. Peacemakers are called to love people. Statements like this can cut deeply into the spirit of a godly leader. Since Paul refuses material support from the Corinthians, his enemies reason that he has something evil hidden up his sleeve, and they want to control him. He refuses to allow it. In love, Paul serves the church not as a puppet having his strings pulled by those with influence, but rather as a man of God, dedicated wholly to his Lord. He refuses to be directed by the false teachers who are opposing him.

Fourth, Paul is accused of being a thief. Gossip is circulating that he has embezzled the church collection for those in Jerusalem (2 Cor. 4:8; 8:20; 12:16; 1 Cor. 16:3).

Fifth, Paul's enemies are denouncing his preaching as unsuccessful and poor (2 Cor. 4:3; 10:10; 11:6). How sad! The young man mentioned earlier in this chapter was attacked for the quality of his preaching. There is good preaching and bad preaching. Preaching done in the power of the Holy Spirit is needed to change lives today. Paul's preaching was under the anointing of God. Do we as peacemakers really believe that our preaching will go unchallenged when it confronts the evils of the age? Preaching that comes from the heart of God will be like a sword penetrating the souls and spirits of sinful people (Heb. 4:12-13). People will react both positively and negatively.

Sixth, Paul is called a coward. He is bold in his writings to the Corinthians, telling them what to do. But when present with them, he seems wimpy in appearance (2 Cor. 10:1-10), contrasting with a popular idea of how a gifted preacher should look and sound. Paul apparently was not a dramatic or popularly charismatic individual. The late-second-century apocryphal Acts of Paul and Thecla describes him as plump and short, with crooked legs, thin hair, eyebrows joining, and a hooked nose. Perhaps he also had bad eyesight (Gal. 6:11). We might call such a person a wimp, but Paul was not wimpy in his leadership.

When ministry is under attack, the enemies of the cross often feel no restraint in destroying anything that gets in their evil ways. The enemies of the cross do not care if truth is violated. That is a major difference between those who seek salvation through the cross, and those who hate the cross and despise its message. The lovers of the true gospel seek the fulfillment of truth in all their lives. Paul's physical weaknesses do not mean that he has the disapproval of God. In fact, Paul declares that God has chosen the weak vessels to proclaim the gospel (1 Cor. 1:27-29; 2 Cor. 4:7).

Seventh, Paul is accused of being false because he refuses to be supported by the church (2 Cor. 11:5-9; 12:12-14). Paul does not accept material benefits from them and thus gives up his apostolic rights to such support, to make sure they do not think he is selling the gospel for profit. He does not want to put any obstacle in the way of the gospel of Christ (1 Cor. 9). In their immaturity, they might think of him as their hired servant, or as a traveling philosopher speaking for money. In Paul's mind, his benefactor is none other than God himself. It is a shame when leaders in a congregation use the purse strings to "keep the pastor in line."

I remember pastoring a church where the treasurer held the check back several days whenever they were mad at me. She played this game to protest the way things were done. How manipulative! Pastors in such a predicament should remember that God is the one who has called them, and God will lead them elsewhere if necessary to support self and family. Woe to the peacemaker who plays that game, trying to keep the appearance of peace, letting others dictate ministry, and not confronting sinners because of that. There is a way to work with others, and there is a way of being a puppet, catering to someone else's prestige or power.

If these were all that Paul had to worry about, they would be enough to absorb his ministry time as he tried to solve them. However, there is more. The Corinthian church has problems regarding the lifestyles and doctrinal issues.

Problems Paul Addresses in the Church

The above accusations against the apostle Paul were external in nature. They were formulated by the enemies of the cross against the gospel itself. They were designed to ruin the integrity of the apostle and to foster false doctrine in the church. Added to these were additional problems the apostle had to address to purify the church.

The internal problems in the Corinthian house churches included threats of church division due to the tensions at hand within the church (1 Cor. 1:10—4:21), incest among those confessing Christianity (5:1-8), fellowship with church members keeping immoral lifestyles and worshiping idols (5:9-13), lawsuits among believers who profess to love each other in Christ (6:1-9a), prostitution (6:9-20), sexual behavior not expressing the love of God (7:1-7), remarriage (7:8-9), divorce (7:10-16), celibacy (7:14-35), marriage (7:25-35), idol-offerings (8:1—11:1), conduct at the Lord's Supper (10:16-22), worship formats (11:2-34), women's veiling (11:2-16), spiritual gifts (12:1—14:40), and misunderstandings concerning the resurrection of the dead (chap. 15).

The Corinthians are not every pastor's dream of the "perfect church." Yet there are many opportunities for ministry if the people will submit to the lordship of Christ.

Responding to Accusations

In conflict resolution it is necessary to investigate each side of the contention to understand the different points of view. At Corinth, the complexity of resolving the problems is increased by the fact that there are several different issues and opponents present in the church. Added to this is the unavailability of documentation from Paul's opponents. We proceed with confidence that the Bible is trustworthy. It is an adventure in Christ to discover what was really happening in that church.

Some would say that our examination is limited since we can only examine the issues from Paul's point of view. If the letters to the Corinthians were only one person's point of view, we would be in trouble. However, this is not the case. The letters to the Corinthians were written after considerable thought and assimilation of the evidence received through encounters with both critical and credible witnesses. Paul writes 1 Corinthians with Sosthenes and 2 Corinthians with Timothy. He refers to other fellow leaders (1 Cor. 1:11-12; 16:10-20; 2 Cor. 7:6, 13). Therefore, the bias of Paul is not the issue at hand. We can proceed, believing that what is said in the Scriptures is true. Paul's description of his opponents provides vital information needed to discover the true issues of the conflict.

The false apostles were opposed to Paul and claimed he had no good leadership with the Corinthians. They insisted that he was not a true apostle. They said he had no right to make judgments concerning the church. The apostle Paul is quick to point out that he has been given a divine mandate to establish the church at Corinth (2 Cor. 10:15-16; Rom. 15:15-20). He declares that he did not build the church on the work of another leader, as his opponents were doing in Corinth. He had gone to Gentiles who had not heard the news of the resurrection of Jesus the Christ. His opponents had infiltrated his work among the Corinthians. They were intruders into Paul's sphere of ministry, which was given to him by the grace of God. They were the evildoers, not Paul.

Paul sees the accusations against his apostolic calling as an assault against the gospel. He is faced with a problem. If he loses credibility as a called apostle of God, then the truths he has taught regarding the gospel are suspect to the Corinthians. If he is not the apostle of the church and divinely appointed by God, then there is no credible reason to recognize his authority within the church.

In each of the Corinthian letters, the introduction declares him to be an apostle, sent by God. His authority rests in the call of God upon his life. God has given him the responsibility of apostleship. He is a representative of God's grace through Jesus Christ. Paul sees no change in his apostolic oversight of Corinth even when he is residing in Ephesus. He recognizes that because of his distance from Corinth, he is somewhat hindered in ministering to the congregation. He also realizes that his apostolic calling is not just limited to the Corinthians. He is apostle for all the church he has served.

As their apostle, he displays his relationship to them with regard to Titus: "As for Titus, he is my partner and co-worker in your service; as for our brothers, they are messengers of the churches, the glory of Christ" (2 Cor. 8:23). Titus has spiritual oversight of many scattered congregations, along with Paul. They are co-workers, communicators of the gospel. God has appointed them for service to the church. Therefore, Paul recognizes the Corinthian crisis as a problem that must be handled by the care of the whole church.

The spiritual life of the whole church is always affected by the spiritual wholeness of any part of it. A bit of sin will destroy the whole body if not dealt with under the leadership appointed by God (1 Cor. 5:6-8). Acts 13:2 reminds us that the Holy Spirit commissioned the church at Antioch to send Paul and Barnabas into ministry. Paul's commission involves the anointing of the Holy Spirit to provide leadership ministry, and the church's recognition of that event. This commissioning is necessary and long-term. It has been given under the sovereignty of almighty

God. The Corinthian opponents of Paul cannot alter or cancel what God has ordained. Division at Corinth causes problems; yet through the apostolic calling, God has already chosen instruments of his, to intervene in his name.

Today, church leaders need to have a fresh understanding of the calling that has been received in people's lives to promote the gospel. Pastors, elders, and deacons should take note of the high calling that God has given them. If this calling is understood, it will lead to boldness in administering the love of God to congregations. In his perfect will, God has chosen to do what will serve his church the best way possible. This is a mystery, yet true. God uses the weak to confound the strong.

The commissioning of Paul will remain intact. The majority of the Corinthians will also recognize and declare comradeship with his co-workers, such as Apollos and Cephas. Each of these leaders and many more are under the authority of Christ to serve his church. The perspective of the opponents is severely limited, keeping them from discerning God's will and the real issues before them. Paul has ministerial duties to perform in the church. He is a declared tool of God, commissioned to lay a foundation upon which the entire church would be built. The foundation is Christ, not Paul himself (1 Cor. 3:11). Whenever people put themselves before Christ and rob him of his rightful glory, they do not walk in his way.

The involvement of Paul is necessitated by the attacks upon the foundation that has already been laid. The true definition of the gospel is at stake. Paul has the right to reenter the church scene at Corinth because he is the church planter and is responsible to maintain a pure gospel there. That gospel stands in opposition to the falsehood of the enemies of the cross. These enemies were not well-intentioned people. They hated the grace of God given to everyone in the teaching of the cross.

Paul's ethical dealings with the congregation exhibit a concern about how the body of Christ is fitted together in love. He announces that each member is to be respected, and all the actions of the church are to rest upon the command to love others as Christ loves them. Paul announces that when one part of the body of Christ suffers, then everyone shares in the suffering. He insists that together we experience joy.

The faithful Corinthians are united in serving the Lord. The intruders are serving their own selfish selves. Paul reminds the believers that the action of God has brought them into spiritual unity. He is convinced that any deed rending that unity must be dealt with through his apostolic office. No member of the church has preeminence over another. Yet there are differences in service. Paul's calling is apostleship. He does not exhibit false pride in his understanding of his calling, but at the same time he does have a high opinion of his office. It is a gift of God's grace to him. His attitude and desire is to live out the calling faithfully before God.

Paul also understands that in his calling he has been made a servant: "What then is Apollos? What is Paul? Servants through whom you came to believe, as the Lord assigned to each" (1 Cor. 3:5). There was a definite time in the past when the Corinthians embraced this understanding. The servants that God used to birth their community are leaders like Paul and Apollos. They are God's agents of redemption. The Lord has given these servants special authorization to use their spiritual gifting in the church. Each one has a part in the development of the church. Neither Apollos nor Paul can take credit for what the Lord has done through them. They are simple servants who do as their Master directs.

Paul requests the Corinthians to view him and his comrades as "servants of Christ and stewards of God's mysteries" (1 Cor. 4:1). He has been judged with the fleshly eyes of his opponents. Paul has not been judged by those with spiritual eyes.

From Paul we receive a revolutionary concept concerning ministry. Ministry is an offensive aimed against the enemies of the cross, to reconcile them to God. That is indeed tough work. He is a partner with the entire church in an attack against spiritual darkness (2 Cor. 5:18; 4:1-5). Together, the church and the apostle are to work against this darkness.

Paul's refusal to boast against his calling is consistent with genuine humility and total reliance upon Christ for the ability to minister. He should not be judged simply by what methods he employs in ministry, but rather by the condition of his heart and the greatness of God's calling. He fulfills his apostleship with godly character and faithful administration of the strategy God has assigned to him. Through his actions, he expresses what he believes. When Paul observes the problems in the church, he responds with a spiritual strategy that will promote true peace.

When a cup of cold water is required for those in need, he takes it one step farther. He is willing not only to provide the water of life for all people; he is also willing to share from the well of Christ's sufferings (Phil. 3:10). Throughout Paul's encounter with the Corinthians, he has suffered. From his heart, he pleads for them, reminding them of their affliction in Asia, the excessive burdens, so that they despaired even of life. "We had received the sentence of death so that we would rely not on ourselves but on God who raises the dead" (2 Cor. 1:9). He says, "I wrote you out of much distress and anguish of heart and with many tears, not to cause you pain, but to let you know the abundant love that I have for you" (2:4). "Make room in your hearts for us; we have wronged no one" (7:2).

Paul painfully endured rejection and suffering for the greater good of the church. In peacemaking, the battle to prove our integrity will not be understood by everyone who enters into our lives. However, God knows perfectly the intent of our heart. He loves us and will provide a means for the emancipation of men and women by the power of the blood of Jesus Christ.

There is also evidence showing the emotional integrity of the apostle. Sometimes the apostle's afflictions were severe. They came from the pressure produced both inside the church and outside of it. In Paul's times of affliction, he learned the importance of not trusting himself, but rather trusting the One who raised Jesus from the dead. He determined to listen to the voice of God, both through the co-workers and members who supported him, and through the working of the Spirit in his life. The Lord told him, "My grace is sufficient for you, for power is made perfect in weakness." So Paul says, "I will boast all the more gladly of my weaknesses, so that the power of Christ may dwell in me" (2 Cor. 12:9).

If Paul's apostleship was indeed peacemaking, then we can conclude that the prerequisite of peacemaking includes positioning oneself before God in spiritual anticipation and brokenness. There must be total reliance on God. This seems to be a key for Paul. To the Philippians he writes, "I want to know Christ and the power of his resurrection and the sharing of his sufferings by becoming like him in his death, if somehow I may attain the resurrection from the dead" (Phil 3:10). His emotional state as well as his ministry is determined by Christ's death and resurrection rather than circumstances with their preconceived grim conclusions. There were times in Paul's brokenness when he was torn apart by personal human pain and inability to achieve his personal goals. He despaired even of life. His hope was directed to the ability of Jesus Christ to deliver him from his burdens.

There was no "I don't care" attitude in Paul. Christ's love compelled him to be involved in the trials of the church and to suffer in that ministry. In stressful situations people often try to minimize the pain of conflict by saying that the conflict is not their problem. The attitude of "I don't care" or "It's not my problem" is often used when there is pain in confronting sensitive issues occurring in the congregation. There is a world of difference between trying to live as a responsible person and denying our own involvement with statements like that. In most cases our responses to problems arise directly from incorrect perceptions of our own ability to solve current issues and relate to other people in crisis.

When we say "It's not my problem" or "Who cares anyway?"

we do not contribute to our own well-being or to finding viable solutions to the problems. If anything, we may add to our own personal guilt from being unable to cope with a given situation. In some circumstances the best course is for us to realize that we are concerned but unable to be involved in settling the crisis because of the nature of the situation. If this thought is truthfully applied to our lives, it may free us of false guilt. We can step back and take a breath of fresh air. Not all problems are ours to solve. Not all problems are our business. There is a time to be actively involved in conflict resolution. There is a time to step back out of the situation.

Sometimes we can safely say, "I am concerned about what is happening, but I do not feel it is in my best emotional and spiritual interest to be involved in the conflict and its resolution." This may be sanctified common sense. This can also be an ideal choice of action before actually becoming involved in a crisis. By stepping back, we can concentrate on waiting upon God for answers without feeling the pressure that we must do something now. In conflict resolution it is always essential to seek God and his grace for spiritual victory.

The battle to establish our own integrity begins with knowing our limitations. Only when necessary and under the guidance of almighty God can we move beyond inactivity to venture into conflict and its heartbreak. We need determination to be intelligent in what we do in conflict resolution. It is foolish to think that we by ourselves can foolhardily and offensively engage the enemy. The key is to be surrendered to Christ. If we truly are his ambassadors, then we must wisely move forward as he leads us.

Jesus Christ once asked whether someone would start to build a house without counting the cost. If we fail to do nothing immediately in a crisis, we sometimes wrongly believe we have done nothing. The truth is that in some situations, when we have done nothing, we may well have done everything by staying out of something that is not our business, in which we have no guidance from God to be involved. We determine our integrity by what we do and don't do. To maintain our personal integrity and thus not to damage the reputation of the gospel, we must be constantly seeking divine guidance and anointing for ministry. Without such an anointing for ministry, we will surely fail.

The Peacemaker Not Working Alone

Paul's involvement with the churches in the ancient world was based on sound biblical principles. First, he understood that peacemaking was a corporate effort involving the entire church. He did not engage in conflict resolution by himself. He depended upon trusted companions. His ability to discern the issues of any crisis grew from the counsel of others. Paul did not rely solely upon his own intuition. He surrounded himself with co-workers who differed in opinions, personality, leadership abilities, and gifting.

Perhaps Paul even received information from the unchurched as the conflict in the church became worse. Chloe and some of her household might not have been converted (1 Cor. 1:11), but they brought word to Paul about divisions in the church at Corinth. Peacemaking demands credible information for grasping the situation. Paul had left Corinth for Ephesus. Now he was an outsider to the congregation. He recognized the importance of receiving as much information as possible from as many credible sources as possible. He had to listen to both the pros and cons of the crisis. Then he had to assimilate the information into responsible action for the cause of Christ. Paul had to personally exhibit self-control in everything he did in response to the evil within the church.

Second, Paul recognized that risks had to be taken. Paul had to trust certain details of the negotiations to others. At times he was not the person who could most effectively resolve the issues. He had to trust young Timothy, who was inexperienced. He had to send Titus, when perhaps he would rather have sent Timothy. Both Timothy and Titus were gifted by God. They were both essential in different levels of resolution. There is an appropriate time for change of task groups. Paul recognized this need in resolution. He knew when Timothy needed rest, and when Titus was alert and ready for peacemaking leadership. He knew when to be there in person and when to be absent from the scene of conflict.

Third, Paul was prepared to deal with the real issues at hand. There is a great difference between what appears to be a problem and what really is the problem. Paul concentrated on what mattered most in the church in relationship to eternity with God. The question was not about loyalty to an inner circle of leadership. The issue was this: What have the Corinthians done with the centrality of the cross in their lives? The cross alone is the eternal beacon of reconciliation with God. All action in the lives of the Corinthians was to be weighed in relationship to that event. Paul defined the cross and proved his devotion to its message of reconciliation. The credibility of peacemaking was greatly affected by the proven character of the peacemaker. Paul could not ignore the attacks on his apostolic authority. To do so would have left his proclamation open to a weak defining of the gospel itself.

The attacks that the apostle Paul experienced were not just against him. They were also directed toward others who loved Jesus and were members of his eternal church. Although no one suffered injustice because of Paul, he knew that others had suffered injustice from the enemies of the cross. A small group of godly participants in the adventure with Jesus teamed up to make a difference in their church. Their common goal was a united church committed totally to Christ. Here is some of the outstanding comradeship they possessed in their teamwork to establish peace in the church.

Titus on the Peacemaking Team

Titus delivered a letter from Paul to the Corinthians that Paul had described as painful (2 Cor. 1:23—2:13; 7:3-16). Before writing the letter, the apostle Paul had encountered opposition and hostility by some of those who falsely claimed they were apostles. To help in the resolution of the problem, Paul sent Titus to visit the Corinthians. Titus, like Timothy, appears as a trusted co-worker. Titus, for unknown reasons, was delayed in returning to Paul. Paul became deeply concerned for him and traveled to meet him in Macedonia. Paul was then informed that the situation at Corinth had momentarily improved. Paul then took advantage of the improved relationships and went personally to Corinth (2 Cor. 8:6, 16-24).

It is apparent that Titus was skilled in working with people and was directly responsible for the positive change. Paul speaks of Titus and his relationship to him and calls him "my partner and co-worker in your service" (2 Cor. 8:23).

Like Paul, Titus was a representative of Christ to many churches. Together they were co-workers in Christ. In all conflict resolution, leaders must recognize that they are cooperating with others in the body of Christ. God expects us to work together for the common good of all. The men and women that Paul gathered around him were communicators of the gospel. They had been appointed for service by the universal church. These servants of Christ saw the Corinthian crisis as a problem that must be handled cooperatively through the care of the wider church.

The body life of the universal church is always affected by the spiritual health of any part of it. We cannot separate ourselves from one another and remain healthy. Acts 13:2 reminds us that the Holy Spirit commissioned the church at Antioch to send Paul and Barnabas into ministry. We need to recognize God-ordained ministry in the church. Paul's debate with the intruders at Corinth was a battle to confirm his ordination by God and the integrity of the gospel.

Timothy on the Peacemaking Team

Paul's relationship to Timothy was more than just being a supervisor of his activity. Timothy was involved in ministry that was deeply affecting people. He was in the heat of the battle. The apostle Paul was deeply concerned for his welfare and urged the church to respect and love him. The conflict at Corinth was emotionally tense. Paul was not just concerned whether Timothy could negotiate a peaceful solution to the problems of the church, but also whether the Corinthians might feel slighted that Paul did not come to the church himself.

There are several things mentioned in the Scriptures concerning the character of Timothy. First, in 2 Timothy 3:14-15, Paul instructs him on how to conduct himself in his ministry before the Lord. Paul is the authoritative figure for Timothy in ministry. Paul's intention is to visit Timothy soon; this suggests a closeness or bonding between them. They considered themselves co-workers together.

Second, in 1 Timothy 4:12-16, Timothy is portrayed as an effective instrument of God in ministry. He was a preacher of God's word in his own right under grace. Timothy was gifted by the Holy Spirit for ministry. Paul instructs him not to neglect his gifting. The relationship of Paul and Timothy shows an eagerness toward cooperative outreach.

Third, in 2 Timothy 1:8, Timothy is encouraged to suffer for Christ. His service to God was sacrificing.

Fourth, in 2 Timothy 2:1-7, Paul considers Timothy to be his own son in the faith. Paul was a spiritual father teaching his spiritual son the discipline of working with the church.

Paul did not always choose to use Timothy in conflict resolution. Titus, rather than Timothy, served as Paul's ambassador in the crisis previously mentioned (2 Cor. 1:23—2:13; 7:5-16). Perhaps Paul thought the intensity of this crisis would be beyond Timothy's abilities at the present time.

Apollos on the Peacemaking Team

Apollos was a gifted orator of God's word. When he first arrived in Corinth, both Priscilla and Aquilla took an interest in his ministry. Since he knew only the baptism of John, they "explained the Way of God to him more accurately." Through this encounter, he apparently received Christian baptism and the Holy Spirit (Acts 18:24-28).

The congregation at Corinth accepted Apollos into their fellowship with great enthusiasm. His preaching was exciting and skillful. Soon some of the Corinthians began to see Apollos as a greater authority than Paul (1 Cor. 1:12). This problem began to increase when Paul's authority as an apostle was challenged by the intruders who were now in the church.

There is no sign that Apollos encouraged this split between those cheering for Paul and those cheering for him. When he left Corinth, he apparently went to Ephesus. Paul had invited him to visit with him (16:12). Some interpreters wonder if he was trying to stay out of the problems at Corinth. We assume that both he and Paul were seeking the overall good of the Corinthians.

Stephanas, Fortunatus, and Achaicus on the Team

These three men traveled to Ephesus from the Corinthian congregation to discuss the tensions in the congregation.

Stephanas was Paul's first convert at Corinth (1 Cor. 16:15). He and his household were soon baptized by the apostle. He traveled with Fortunatus and Achaicus, bringing fresh information about the crisis. Possibly they carried Paul's first letter home to Corinth. Stephanas was strongly commended by Paul as one worthy of exercising leadership in the church. He had devoted himself to the ministry of the saints (16:15-16).

Priscilla and Aquila on the Peacemaking Team

Priscilla and Aquila were married. They were expelled from Rome under the edict of the emperor Claudius. They met Paul in Corinth. It is not known if they were converted before they left Rome or after they met Paul in Corinth. When Paul left Corinth, they journeyed with him to Ephesus (1 Cor. 16:19). Aquilla is also mentioned in Romans (16:3). Apparently they later returned to Rome to proclaim the gospel of Christ.

Chloe's Household on the Peacemaking Team

The household of Chloe informed the apostle Paul of the disharmony at Corinth (1 Cor. 1:11). It is doubtful that Chloe was of the Corinthian fellowship. It may also be that she did part of her business in Corinth, and thus came upon the news of disharmony within the congregation. Some think her home was actually in Ephesus. Through her contact in Corinth or through her servants, she learned firsthand what was happening in the church. There is no clear evidence that she was a Christian. This part of her life is unknown.

In 1 Corinthians, Paul seems to respect what Chloe's people told him. He learned much about the focus of the division in the church. He apparently believed their testimony was credible. The three-man delegation sent from the church to Paul might be prejudiced in their witness. Chloe could be a source of reliable information to him. She was an outsider to the Corinthian congregation.

Peacemakers Need Anointing by the Holy Spirit

Throughout this book I have stressed that successful conflict resolution must depend on the intervention of God. Human methodology cannot supersede or replace the need for God to be working personally in the affairs of our lives. God has purposed in himself to reconcile people to a true state of peace that is not dependent upon outward circumstances, but rather on the indwelling presence of God in us.

When I first began to look for ways to bring healing to troubled congregations in which I pastored, I was looking for methodology. Methodology is what I didn't need. Methodology that is divorced from divine involvement is doomed from its very inception. I thought if I learned to pray a little harder or work longer, then I could bring resolution to the church.

The methodology of God involves much more than work. It means coming to grips with our own spirituality. It involves a character change in our own lives as we learn to yield to Christ.

Peacemaking begins in our lives when we first discover that the grace of God is transforming us and will continue to transform us into the character of Christ. It is easy to plan strategies for peacemaking. However, it is a greater undertaking to discover strategy that is dependent upon God. This is the highest adventure. In submission to Christ, the peacemaker personally encounters the need to die to self and to live in the power of the Holy Spirit. There is no substitute for a hunger for the things of God in the life of any would-be peacemaker.

Peacemakers recognize the impossibility of triumphing over sin apart from grace. They realize that the only methodology that will work is centered in absolute reliance upon God to change the condition of human hearts. The peacemaker must be under the total control of almighty God, personally experiencing the Holy Spirit's filling and baptism.

The ministry of the Holy Spirit supplies two essential ingredients necessary for credible peacemaking. First, the discovery and realization of personal purity. How can impure persons lead others to purity in conflict resolution unless they first experience purity themselves? True biblical peacemaking must be pure. God is pure, and he bestows purity upon his servants. Through the grace of God, we are cleansed from all sin. The ultimate goal of conflict resolution is cleansing from sin.

Deciding who is on what side in a controversy is not important. In any situation, the issue is this: Who is on the Lord's side? When all parties in conflict discover heart purity for their lives, then the peacemakers will find rejoicing and satisfaction in their role in the church. Second, the Holy Spirit grants believers spiritual power not only to triumph over sin but also to transform any given situation from defeat to spiritual emancipation as we are set free by Christ.

The apostle Peter wrote, "As he who called you is holy, be holy yourselves in all your conduct" (1 Pet. 1:15). The Holy Spirit's work enables the Christian to no longer resemble the evils of the world. The believer represents the purity and power of the Lord God himself.

You may recall in the first chapter how eighty pastors were asked what they would do if they were called to minister in a church in crisis. Many of those pastors said they would pray more. When I first heard those statements, I admit that I was concerned. Part of me thought at least subconsciously that they were hiding from the reality of the situation rather than confronting it directly. I wanted a foolproof methodology. I believed in prayer, but subconsciously I wanted to make things happen.

Notice that I said I wanted to make things happen. This attitude is far from the heart of God. He wants us to discover how to be weak vessels who are useful to him. God wants to make things happen. God has provided a way, through enhancement of our spirituality by the Spirit's ministry. Prayer is the beginning of discovering the answer. True prayer is meant to create intimate fellowship with God. It must be developed. Sin breaks our fellowship with God. The person who is desperate to be a peacemaker must discover the greatness of prayer. Peacemakers must learn the reality of living in the presence of Christ. The daily grind can be put aside in prayer communion. In prayer we can enter the throne room of the universe.

Many Christians find prayer uncomfortable in their early stages of growth. However, the more we spend time in this fellowship with God, the greater the anointing we will experience in our lives. If our goal is to reflect the love of Christ, then we must seek his transformational anointing which comes through the Holy Spirit. This will accelerate us into a new ministry.

The sufferings of peacemakers, their spiritual brokenness, the work of grace in their lives—these are all tools used by God to make us more Christlike. The baptism of the Holy Spirit grants Christ's character as a marvelous endowment for the good of the church. The Holy Spirit seals us in Christ's redemption and empowers us to declare the divine Peacemaker, the Prince of Peace.

The man or woman who discovers this empowerment from God will find strength granted to them in the struggles to establish the peace of the kingdom of God. This is a mandate from God for all believers.

Summary

The servants of the Lord who wish to establish peace among people need to be aware of what they will experience in their struggles for peace.

1. There are no pat answers in conflict resolution. Peacemakers must realize that their task is difficult. Their search for spiritual answers to human problems will begin in their own life. They will find spiritual freedom from sin if they truly search with all their heart. They cannot help others in the fullness of the power of God until they have personally discovered freedom from sin.

2. Peacemakers must be prepared to ask themselves hard personal questions about their own involvement in the conflict. God will provide assistance and comfort for peacemakers as they search for answers. Their answers will not always be comfortable ones. Some will tax peacemakers into brokenness before God.

3. Peacemakers must seek spiritual discernment to know what they are doing right and what they are doing wrong. Their task is to search for the heart of God in every conflict.

4. Peacemakers must be prepared to defend their personal integrity lest the gospel itself be scorned by the enemies of the cross. Peacemakers share a common suffering with others. They must be able to critically diagnose the accusations of opponents. In conflict there will be many who will not understand us or our efforts in peacemaking.

APPENDIX

Sample Problems

Exercise in Conflict Resolution

Throughout this book you have been given opportunity to expand your thinking with regard to conflict resolution and the church. In this appendix are two settings of church-related problems for you to solve. These settings relate to information given above. Evaluate what you have read and put it into action. The goal of this exercise is to help you be better able to handle a church crisis.

Case Study: The Old Stone Church

The Old Stone Church has a rich heritage, but it is not what it used to be. The old-timers remember the great revival of 1956 when lots of people found Christ. Several were called into full-time service. In fact, Elder Jones often testifies of his conversion when Pastor Smith was anointed by the Spirit. He says, "No one has ever been anointed to preach like him on that there night."

However, things have changed in forty years. The church council is now ready to give up on the church and any possible future that it may have for their community. No one wants to pastor the church. They have been hunting for a pastor for nearly a year. Meanwhile, they have had four part-time student pastors in four years. The last one left after only four months.

In 1954, there were 154 persons attending the church each week. Now there are only twenty-five. People have come and gone from the church. Most have left because of elder Jones. He has a habit of being an old stick in the mud. Whenever someone has an idea about moving the church forward, he brings up some nice-sounding reason to delay the plans. Some believe that he controls the church. He does. He is related to just about everybody in the church except you. Few people want to cross paths with him. Even though he controls most things in the church, many have been secretly at odds with him for years.

There is an undertow in the congregation that no one wants to speak about openly. You have been greatly burdened for the church. You are relatively new to the congregation.

What can be done to help this congregation? Is there any hope for this church? Why so? Why not? Is this church dead? What should you expect if a full-grown battle is waged over your peacemaking efforts?

Case Study: The South Side Interdenominational Evangelical Assembly of the Living Gospel Church

You are an active member of the church. In mid-July the pastor asks you to collect the offering and deliver it to Mrs. Smith. She is the church treasurer and related to everyone in the church. She is on vacation and will not be in church that Sunday. You followed the pastor's instructions. You have even counted the offering of $1,964.72. You wrote the amount down on your bulletin to tell Mrs. Smith later. However, when you gave her the offering the following Monday, you forget to tell her you counted it. A month later the pastor asked you to do it again. You counted the offering, and it was $1,734.59. You again write down the figure.

When the congregation had its quarterly meeting in October, Mrs. Smith presented the treasurer's report to the congregation. She said that the giving to the church is less than what is needed to pay the bills. The congregation was given a verbal report. However, on the written report for the Sundays that you collected the offerings, you saw a discrepancy. A total of $750.00 was missing.

The following morning you called Pastor Brown and told

him what you knew about the report. He assured you that Mrs. Smith was an excellent treasurer, and immediately he dropped the subject. But afterward, you can't forget there is money missing. In accord with Matthew eighteen, you quietly went to Mrs. Smith during the week and asked her if there was a mistake. She assured you that there was none. You then told her that you counted the money. She was outraged at you and ordered you out of her house. On the next Sunday morning, the entire congregation is in an uproar. She has told everyone that you have called her a thief. The truth is that you were extremely courteous when you spoke to her. The majority of the church is mad at you.

What should you do? What assurances should you expect from God in the way of help for you? What must you do in **relationship** to Mrs. Smith?

SELECT BIBLIOGRAPHY

Augsburger, David W. *The Love Fight*. Scottdale, Pa.: Herald Press, 1973; rev. ed., *Caring Enough to Confront*. 1980. Ventura, Calif.: Regal Books, 1981.

_____. *When Caring Is Not Enough: Resolving Conflicts Through Fair Fighting*. Ventura, Calif.: Regal Books, 1983. Scottdale, Pa.: Herald Press, 1983.

Bolton, Robert. *People Skills*. New York: Simon & Schuster, 1979.

Bossart, Donald E. *Creative Conflict in Religious Education and Church Administration*. Birmingham: Religious Education Press, 1980.

Carson, Donald A. *From Triumphalism to Maturity: An Exposition of 2 Corinthians 10-13*. Grand Rapids: Baker Book House, 1984.

Crabb, Lawrence M., and Dan B. Allender. *Encouragement: The Key to Caring*. Grand Rapids: Zondervan, 1984.

Douglas, Lewis. *Resolving Church Conflicts*. San Francisco: Harper & Row, 1981.

Flynn, Leslie B. *Great Church Fights*. Wheaton: Victor Books, 1973.

Fox, George. *The Journal of George Fox*. Ed. John L. Nickalls. London: Religious Society of Friends, 1975.

Haugk, Kenneth C. *Antagonist in the Church*. Minneapolis: Augsburg, 1988.

Heggen, Carolyn Holderread. *Sexual Abuse in Christian Homes and Churches*. Scottdale, Pa.: Herald Press, 1993.

Henderson, Robert T. *A Door of Hope: Spiritual Conflict in Pastoral Ministry*. Scottdale, Pa.: Herald Press, 1997.

Kittlaus, Paul, and Speed B. Leas. *Church Fights: Managing Conflict in the Local Church.* Louisville: Westminster John Knox, 1973.

Jeschke, Marlin. *Discipling in the Church: Recovering a Ministry of the Gospel.* Scottdale, Pa.: Herald Press, 1988.

Leas, Speed B. *Leadership and Conflict.* Creative Leadership Series. Nashville: Abingdon, 1982.

――――――. *Moving Your Church Through Conflict.* Bethesda, Md.: Alban Institute, 1985.

Lewis, Douglas G. *Resolving Church Conflicts.* San Francisco: Harper & Row, 1981.

Lloyd, Perry M., and Gilbert A. Peterson. *Churches in Crisis.* Chicago: Moody, 1981.

McCollough, Charles R. *Resolving Conflict with Justice and Peace.* New York: Pilgrim, 1991.

McSwain, Larry L., and William C. Treadwell. *Conflict Ministry in the Church.* Nashville: Broadman, 1981.

Miller, John M. *The Contentious Community: Constructive Conflict in the Church.* Philadelphia: Westminster, 1978.

Parsons, George, and Speed B. Leas. *Intervening in a Church Fight: A Manual for Internal Consultants.* Bethesda, Md.: Alban Institute, 1996.

Peck, M. Scott. *A Different Drum.* New York: Simon & Schuster, 1987.

Shawchuck, Norman. *How to Manage Conflict in the Church.* 2 vols. Irvine, Calif.: Organization Resource Press, 1986.

Shelly, Marshall. *Well-Intentioned Dragons.* Waco, Tex.: Word, 1985.

Toews, John, with Eleanor Loewen. *No Longer Alone: Mental Health and the Church.* Scottdale, Pa.: Herald Press, 1995.

White, John, and Ken Blue. *Healing the Wounded: The Costly Love of Church Discipline.* Downers Grove, Ill.: InterVarsity, 1985.

Yoder, John Howard. "Binding and Loosing." In *Body Politics: Five Practices of the Christian Community Before the Watching World.* Nashville, Tenn.: Discipleship Resources, 1992.

THE AUTHOR

Dave Peters has served in pastoral ministry in the Evangelical Friends Church, Eastern Region, since 1976. He served in a series of churches torn apart by division that originated before he assumed leadership. Peters says that in the heartbreaks of conflict, God molds servants given to obedience to God.

He daily searches for intimacy with God. His passion is for peacemaking. Peters loves to participate in the creating of new devotion among Christians who previously have been alienated from each other. His loving concern for people allows for a safe pastoral encounter to bring people together.

He holds a B.A. degree from Malone College, Canton, Ohio, and a M.Div. from Ashland (Ohio) Theological Seminary. He has taken part in Doctor of Ministry programs at Nazarene Theological Seminary, Kansas City, Missouri (1983-86), and Ashland Theological Seminary (1990-91).

Peters is a native of Cleveland and now resides in Youngstown, Ohio, with his wife, Barbara Ann, and three children, Jonathan David, Rebecca Lynn, and Elijah Daniel.